"Kathleen Nielson examines hard questions about women and God that some might be afraid to ask: Is God for women? Does he like us? Using God's own words in Scripture, Nielson teaches us that the answer is a resounding 'Yes!'"

Colleen J. McFadden, Director of Women's Workshops,
Charles Simeon Trust

"I have started to read loads of books on women, but this one is unique—partly because I finished it! In fact I couldn't put it down. Kathleen has gathered all the tricky questions about women and tackles them head-on. Equipped with a unique blend of experience and insight into what it's like to be a woman in today's culture, Kathleen gives thoroughly biblical answers, pointing us to the gospel on every page. As I read about what I was created for, I was moved to tears and felt a burden lift from my shoulders. Every chapter brings fresh insights as Kathleen unflinchingly grapples with tricky verses. It's simple, accessible, up to date and down to earth, and is a book I will keep coming back to."

Linda Allcock, London Women's Convention

"Some theological debaters become terribly shrill—both in their treatment of Scripture and of each other. In our day, debate over the treatment of women, especially in the church, is one of the hot topics. I hope that many readers on all sides of this debate will take the time and invest the energy to listen carefully and respectfully to Kathleen, a woman who has a keen mind, a heart devoted to Scripture, and the courtesy to treat other viewpoints fairly even while she marshals the evider   understanding of key passages and th   hard questions," and she is s

D.A. Carson, Re   rinity
Evangelical Divinity Schoc   ilition

"Kathleen Nielson proficiently unpacks difficult passages of Scripture that we sometimes want to avoid. On every page, she helps us wrestle with complex questions, while inviting us to embrace this beautiful truth: God is good to women. This is an excellent and needed book—I highly recommend it for both men and women."

Melissa Kruger, author of *The Envy of Eve* and
Walking with God in the Season of Motherhood

"At a time when there is increasing confusion and perhaps resistance to God's word about gender, Kathleen offers a clear and wise path to understanding God's word rightly in this important area. She carefully explores passages addressing our identity, our worth, and our responsibilities in God's world. Yet don't be fooled into thinking this is a book just for women. This is an excellent resource for men as well, as we all grapple with the Bible's teaching on what it means to be a woman."

Kara Hartley, Archdeacon for Women's Ministry,
Diocese of Sydney, Australia

"I have enjoyed reading this reassuring, satisfying book, which touches on many controversial issues that relate to Christian women. I applaud Kathleen Nielson's courage in facing some difficult questions head-on and I think many will benefit from her thorough approach and carefully argued insights. I especially appreciate her insistence that all our questions on womanhood (and indeed on any subject) must begin with God. Often the issues dealt with in this book are fraught with emotion, which obscures careful reasoning. Kathleen keeps us fixed on the word of God, while showing his love and compassion toward women."

Wendy Virgo, author of *Influential Women* and international speaker

"It is with great joy that I recommend *Women and God*. What I like most about this book is not that it is written by a woman for women but that it is written by a faithful Bible-teacher who happens to be a woman. Kathleen answers the hard questions the Bible raises in relation to women by showing us the beauty of the truths of Scripture and the glory of our Savior, Jesus."

Juan Sanchez, Senior Pastor, High Pointe Baptist Church,
Austin, Texas

"I am encouraged by this book, which takes on a subject that is not easy or popular as it grapples with some seriously hard questions and helps equip us to answer them from God's word. As you read the book, it is easy to see that Kathleen herself delights in the goodness of God's plan for women as she carefully and winsomely seeks to show us how that goodness runs throughout the whole Bible."

Andrea Trevenna, Associate Minister for Women,
St Nicholas, Sevenoaks, UK; author of *The Heart of Singleness*

"I was deeply helped by reading *Women and God*. It is a book written by a wise woman, and it does not shy away from hard, painful, complex issues. Frankly, there are few people I trust more than Dr. Nielsen to push me, challenge me, and make me think rigorously, carefully, and biblically about these things. This book is faithful and sensitive, truthful and persuasive, restrained yet comprehensive, and Kathleen is alert (and sympathetic) to the questions that surround these issues in the church and the world today. She speaks with a woman's experience, and with a desire to help us be faithful to God's word, and to see the goodness of God both in who he created women to be and in what he calls them to do."

Ligon Duncan, Chancellor, Reformed Theological Seminary,
Jackson, Mississippi

"I loved this book! *Women and God* is more than just an overview of the roles of women in the family and the church. It tackles all the usual texts as well as the more shocking and perplexing ones that other people sometimes avoid. Kathleen anticipates all the questions and objections that people have, and then answers them from the text with wisdom, clarity, and sensitivity. What makes this book so compelling is her conviction that God is good, and that women can have confidence that living by his word is a beautiful thing and for our good."

Carrie Sandom, Director of Women's Ministry, The Proclamation Trust, London; Associate Minister for Women at St John's, Tunbridge Wells, UK

"In *Women and God*, we find a writer well prepared to walk through the interior world of godly women who are in need of good answers. In reading it, I had the sense that Kathleen Nielson's voice will encourage, assist, and support Christian women who have reason to feel that the goodness of God has escaped them."

David Helm, Lead Pastor, Holy Trinity Church, Hyde Park, Chicago; Chairman, The Simeon Trust

KATHLEEN NIELSON

Women & God

HARD QUESTIONS.
Beautiful Truth.

thegoodbook
COMPANY

Women & God. *Hard Questions, Beautiful Truth*
© Kathleen Nielson, 2018

Published by:
The Good Book Company

Tel (US): 866 244 2165
Tel (UK): 0333 123 0880
Email (US): info@thegoodbook.com
Email (UK): info@thegoodbook.co.uk

Websites:
North America: www.thegoodbook.com
UK: www.thegoodbook.co.uk
Australia: www.thegoodbook.com.au
New Zealand: www.thegoodbook.co.nz

Unless indicated, all Scripture references are taken from the HOLY BIBLE, NEW INTERNATIONAL VERSION. Copyright © 2011 Biblica, Inc.™ Used by permission.

ISBN: 9781784982799 | Printed in Denmark

Design by André Parker

To my mother.

*One of those holy women
who hope in God.*

(1 PETER 3 v 5-6)

Contents

Introduction   11

1: How We Got Here *Genesis 1*   17

2: Second Place? *Genesis 2*   31

3: Fallen Women *Genesis 3*   45

4: The Darkest Places   61
    Deuteronomy 21; Judges 11 & 19

5: Strong Women *Judges 4 – 5*   77

6: Women, Sex, and a Question   93
    of Double Standards
    Deuteronomy 22; Hosea 1 – 3; John 7 v 53 – 8 v 11

7: Women's Bodies   109
    Psalm 139; 1 Samuel 1 – 2; Luke 1

8: A Man Unlike Any Other *The Gospels*   125

9: Women and Marriage   139
    Ephesians 5 v 21-33; 1 Corinthians 11 v 3-12

10: Women and the Church   157
    1 Corinthians 11 & 14; 1 Timothy 2 v 11-15;
    Titus 2 v 3-5; Romans 16

11: The Goodness of God   173
    1 Timothy 2 v 9-15; 1 Peter 3 v 1-6

Acknowledgments   187

Introduction

One title proposed initially for this book was *Is God Sexist?* I voted thumbs down on that—first of all because I wasn't sure God would like it (even though he knew what my answer would be), and second, because it seemed too much like a set-up. Obviously the answer was going to be "No."

But that question is good to acknowledge, because it gets at the heart of this book, which is to ask how the God Christians believe in views women, and to address fears that he may not view them entirely positively. Voices around us can feed these fears. Public discourse often lumps Christianity in the general category of "religions," in discussions of sexism—that is, unfair attitudes or treatment based on one's biological sex. In one blog article from *The Huffington Post* condemning sexism toward women, first on the list of culprits is "religious sexism and discrimination."[1] The author cites the "ritualized silencing of women" practiced by "all major religions which, with minor exceptions, bar girls and women from ministerial leadership." The result, according to this blog writer?

---

1 Soraya Chemaly, "10 Everyday Sexisms and What We Can Do About Them." http://bit.ly/1tTRNhh. Posted on 7/31/2014. Accessed 9/26/2017.

"Access to the divine is mediated exclusively by men and their speech," and females from the earliest ages learn that their voices are "powerless and not respected."

This book is not an answer to the world's voices. Perhaps you're a follower of Jesus Christ—or perhaps you would like to be. This book speaks to you and to any who want to explore further God's own words about the female human beings he made. The voices around us can be troubling. Blogs can be loud. Many people who believe in Jesus, or who would believe in Jesus, struggle to hold that belief together with what they hear the Bible says about women; a lot of negative things are to be heard. People read a lot of books on what the Bible says about women—and I have hesitated to add to that list! As the wise writer of Ecclesiastes wrote, "Of making many books there is no end..." (Ecclesiastes 12 v 12).

So many women I know are talking about this issue, in one way or another. We need to talk about it. The subject of women and God is not just theoretically crucial; it's personally crucial, for both women and men. I deal with it all the time, both privately and publicly—in my family and church life, in ministry as a Bible teacher, and regularly in conversations with other women:

What does it mean for me that every human being is created in the image of God? How should I process those Old Testament passages where women are so mistreated? Why should I or shouldn't I teach this church class, or take this course of study? How do I deal with the charge that teaching submission leads to abuse of women? What does my faith have to do with my longing for children, or my having children, or my losing children?

Is God sexist?

This book does not ask or answer all the possible questions; it does seek to address some of the hardest ones, by pointing us to listen well to God's voice.

By "God" I'm referring in this book to the God of the Bible, the One who reveals himself through the 66 books of the Old and New Testaments. If what the Bible says is true—that God made the world, and God came into the world to restore the world—then nothing else in the universe is more important than knowing this God. All questions and answers start with him. Gender-related issues are crucial to address—but the first and foremost question must be about God himself: what shall we say about the God who made us, in relation to these issues? As we consider this question, I'm going to assume that the Bible is true. I'm going to take the Scriptures of the Old and New Testaments as what they claim to be—God's breathed-out word to the world, utterly authoritative and fully sufficient for all we believe and do (2 Timothy 3 v 14-17).

If you're someone who doesn't share these assumptions, I invite you to keep reading, and to feel warmly welcomed as a visitor to a biblical perspective. I hope you'll find the Scriptures both beautiful and piercing. If you do share these assumptions, I invite you to listen again to God's word, as I have tried to do, asking God by his Spirit to help us hear his voice ever more clearly. If your time is limited and you must choose between reading this book and reading the Bible, choose the Bible. Read it all the way through. Read and study it with God's people. Take in those life-giving words. They are "words of delight" and "words of truth . . . given by one Shepherd," says that same wise writer of Ecclesiastes. And he adds a warning: to "beware of anything beyond these" (Ecclesiastes 12 v 10-12, ESV).

With that warning in our ears, our method will be to listen closely to God's word through a series of key biblical passages that relate explicitly to women. I wish there were time to develop these passages more fully, but the aim will be to hear them well in context, and through them to discern God's heart and mind specifically in relation to women. We'll move through the Bible from beginning to end, for the Scriptures tell a unified story, and we cannot understand any part without paying attention to the whole. Even as we approach each passage in its immediate context, inevitably we'll need to make some jumps from one part of the Scriptures to another—especially from Old Testament to New. The Bible's one story tells of God redeeming a people for himself through his Son, the Lord Jesus Christ. Any question about God's relation to the people he created is a question that from the beginning fully involves God's Son.

Even as we make progress, all of us still see dimly; we're on our way to seeing Jesus face to face, but we're not there yet. I hope this book will encourage you—even if you don't agree with everything in it—to dig into God's word more deeply. Working on it has certainly challenged and convicted me to do so. I'm hugely grateful for many wise encouragers and leaders who have not only helped me learn but also challenged me to work as hard as possible in my own study. We mustn't be satisfied with second-hand convictions, parroting a system of values or rules, from any source. That will convince no one, including ourselves. God's word is living and active, and through it God's Spirit opens our eyes and hearts, and gradually changes us into the image of Christ.

A spoiler alert is not needed for me to tell you that I'm out to show the goodness of the God who made us—specifically the goodness of God to his female image-bearers. This book is not simply about setting out the truth, but seeking to show how that truth is good and can therefore be welcomed and enjoyed, not simply accepted. I find—and I hope you will, too—that as we wrestle with the hard questions about God and women, we discover some beautiful truths. I'm praying that when you're done reading, you'll be loving and thanking God for the way in which he has created us as gendered human beings. I'm praying you'll be more ready to speak clearly, compassionately, and helpfully with others who are asking questions about women in relation to God—perhaps others who differ in perspective, or who have questions about Scripture's teachings, or who are struggling to trust God in painful circumstances. And I'm praying you'll be more enthralled with the goodness of God's word, and of the Savior at its center.

How We Got Here

B efore we ask what to do about where we are, we need to ask how we got here. The past makes a difference.

If there is a God who created us human beings, then our relationship with that God must be the most important thing in the universe. And if that God created us as male and female, then we need to ask what our Creator thinks about these male and female creatures he made. It's an urgent question. Voices all around us are speaking to issues of gender and sex and sexism; in the midst of the swirl of opinions we need to know how God regards us as men and women. But we need more than that. We need to hear God speak to us personally, as the beings he created and loves and knows, down to each hair on our heads and each organ of our bodies. And we need to respond to him. This book isn't about theory. It's about how we live, because it's about who we are.

As we ask what God says specifically about women in the Bible, it's important to remember that most of the Bible isn't about women; the Bible is about the God who made women and men and who saves them through his Son. The psalms and prayers of the Bible are not gender-specific; every human being cries out to God in praise or lament or worship. The majority of God's commands and promises are not gender-specific; we're all called to love God, to believe in his Son, and to trust the power of the risen Christ in us through the Holy Spirit. And yet there is this distinct reality of maleness and femaleness that appears at the Bible's start and works its way right through to the end. Why? What does this mean?

These questions are hard and sometimes even painful, because we have an understandable fear that making distinctions harms women. I am writing, and you are reading, in a world where women have been and still often are harmed by men. We have only to look at human history, including the history of the church, to find patterns of women being treated unfairly and unlovingly. We rightly work hard to distance ourselves from past prejudices— that is, pre-judgments about women that are not based on reality and that have been used to hold back and harm deeply half of the human race.

Because of prejudice, for centuries women were not allowed to own property or participate in political processes: people pre-judged that women as a whole category were either not smart enough or not valuable enough to bear those responsibilities. In some cultures still today, women are not allowed to share the privileges open to men in areas such as politics and education; girls and women are pre-judged as inferior and unfit. In cultures that have progressed beyond such overt inequalities, prejudices still lurk. To take just one example, a friend of mine in the process of earning a graduate degree was asked by one of her professors whether all the work was worth it, considering both the job market and the fact that she would probably just go on to have children and raise a family. Throughout the world, the human race is still combating the ingrained effects of powerful prejudices from centuries past.

To battle prejudice, we instinctively seek to move forward, letting go of wrongful judgments and practices. Too often, however, the Bible becomes part of what is let go. The Old Testament especially is full of stories in which we seem to recall women who are not treated or valued well. The New Testament seems to contain instructions in which women are treated with prejudice. The old prejudices must go, the thinking runs, so that the new equality may come.

But here's the irony: in order to move forward in the human story, we have to go back to the beginning to find the way. In order to ask what to do about where we are and where we're headed, we do indeed have to find out how we got here. What if the problem is not that people are holding on to judgments that are too old, but to judgments that are *not old enough*?

The long-ago past makes a difference to everything. In fact, the opening chapters of the Bible tell us that everything and everybody today is pre-judged—but not by a human being, and not in a way that oppresses, but that blesses. In order to begin to grasp this, we have to go back to the beginning and to the only one who is perfectly capable of judging anything or anybody. We have to go back to the God who made everything, including us.

In order to talk about the creation of humanity we so often zoom right into Genesis 1 v 27. That verse is where we indeed must go:

> *So God created mankind in his own image,*
> *in the image of God he created them;*
> *male and female he created them.*[2]

---

2 Quoted from the New International Version (2011). Unless noted, Scripture quotations will be from this version. It is worth noting here that Genesis 1 v 27 is rendered differently in the more literal English Standard Version:

But let's first revel for a moment in the huge opening chapter of the Bible. Here are the roots to our human story. Here are the beginnings of the answers to the things we long to know: where we came from, who we are, and how we fit into this swirling life flow in which we find ourselves carried along. This is the front bookend of the whole story, and if we don't set it in place, we can't make sense of our part in it.

Creation with Distinction

I vaguely remember studying mitosis in high school, though I had to download a YouTube video to refresh my memory of this process in which one cell divides into two.[3] The first cell's mass of swirling DNA molecules splits and lines up in two strands of paired chromosomes, which are then pulled apart by two opposite sets of hairy-looking microtubules. With these now two sets of cell matter, the original cell finally divides to form two completely new cells—amazing!

Reading the Bible's opening chapter is like watching a large-scale drama of mitosis. What's so striking is that the whole process of new life emerging, both on the microcellular and the macro Genesis-1 level, is a process of systematic separation and distinction. In thirty-one verses, the Bible's opening chapter takes us from an initial stage of darkness and formlessness through a sovereignly ordered series of creations and divisions: first, light, separated from darkness (v 3-5); then the sky, separated from surrounding waters (v 6-8); and then land, separated from seas (v 9-10).

So God created man in his own image,
  in the image of God he created him;
    male and female he created them.

3 youtube.com/watch?v=C6hn3sA0ip0. Accessed 9/26/2017.

All this division doesn't happen in eerie silence, or with some unnamed narrator, as it does in the YouTube video that refreshed my memory. It happens as the Creator God makes it happen; he is the starting point of the whole story: "In the beginning God created the heavens and the earth" (Genesis 1 v 1). His word is the action; we can't miss the insistent repetition of "And God said" or "Then God said" (v 3, 6, 9, 11, 14, 20, 24, 26, 28, 29). His words not only narrate; they create.

By his word the ordered distinctions continue, as the Creator fills the places he has created. First, plants and trees fill the earth, three times carefully described as bearing seeds and fruit each according to its kind (v 11-13). The order is insistent and beautiful. Next, the sun and moon and stars fill the sky, with the two great lights not only separating the day from the night, but also "governing" in their own distinct spheres: the greater light to rule the day, and the lesser light along with the stars to rule the night (v 14-19). Then begins the filling of the sea and sky and land with living creatures, all in their own places and seven times distinguished as according to their own kinds (v 20-25).

Here at the start of the Bible, before we come to know our own beginnings, we're first of all getting to know God. He is the only source of life. It's all derived from him, and it's all ordered by him—every part of the universe distinguished in its appropriate place and designed according to his word. From the Creator God there pours out this amazing ordered pattern of life and blessing. This is what God is like, from the beginning. When we get to the end of the Bible and glimpse God's throne in heaven, it is this glorious God of creation that all those around the throne are praising:

You are worthy, our Lord and God,
  to receive glory and honor and power,
for you created all things,
  and by your will they were created
  and have their being. (Revelation 4 v 11)

Creation's Climax

God not only creates and separates and fills; he also judges. Repeatedly throughout the narrative, he stops, looks, and gives his verdict as he says that what he has made is "good" (Genesis 1 v 4, 10, 12, 18, 21, 25). His word has created and shaped his creation perfectly, in a sovereignly ordered pattern that leads logically and beautifully to the final piece, the climactic creation. Each new step of creation begins with God saying, "Let"—from "Let there be light" (v 3) to "Let the land produce living creatures" (v 24). This pattern culminates with a distinction in verse 26, as God now says, "Let us make mankind in our image, in our likeness."

This final step in creation is the same, but different. Again we hear "Let," but this time it is "Let us" (v 26). Many commentators believe the "us" gives an early hint of the Trinity: one God in three Persons, in effect having a conversation with himself. The Spirit of God was introduced in verse 1: "The Spirit of God was hovering over the waters." And the New Testament makes clear that "in the beginning" with God was "the Word"—the Word who "was with God, and [who] was God," and who would one day, in human history, be made flesh: Jesus, the Son of God (John 1 v 1, 14, 17). It's this three-personed God—Father, Son, and Spirit—who says, "Let us make mankind in our image."

The primary and entirely unique fact about the creation of mankind, stated three times in Genesis 1 v 26-27, is that God created mankind in his own image. What does this mean? Genesis 1 shows us at least two initial answers to that question.

First, to be made in God's image appears to involve representing his authority, his rule over creation. We've watched God make the seas and the planets, and tell them where to stay and what to do: God rules his creation. But God also spreads his rule throughout that creation—as we saw with the sun and the moon, made to "rule over the day and over the night" (v 18, ESV). God's words, "Let us make mankind in our image," are linked logically to his stated purpose that humanity will rule, or "have dominion," over the other creatures (v 26). God's first record-ed speech to his newly-created human creatures includes a command not only to fill the earth, but also to "subdue it": "Rule over the fish in the sea and the birds in the sky and over every living creature that moves on the ground" (v 28). Human beings made in God's image are not to rule as God, but to rule as God's representatives, with his del-egated authority: they are to rule *like he does*. They are dis-tinct from the rest of creation, made to steward and rule over it together.

So when farmers figure out how best to cultivate the ground to make it fertile and fruitful, bringing forth the most abundant crops year after year, humanity is imaging God in ruling over his creation. When scientists figure out the chemical compounds of penicillin and other life-pre-serving medicines, humanity is imaging God in ruling over his creation. When members of a choir join their voices to create something beautiful with words and melody, they are together imaging God their Creator. Any time a family grows and cultivates order and harmony in its little plot of living space on this planet, they image God in ruling over his creation. (I have shared this truth with growing boys in relation to living spaces such as their bedrooms; it actually helps, sometimes.)

All this leads right to the second point: To be made in God's image appears to involve reflecting his relational nature, the "us" of our three-personed God. Read again those three lines in verse 27:

> *So God created mankind in his own image,*
> *in the image of God he created them;*
> *male and female he created them.*

These are not three unrelated statements. Nor is God just being repetitive. What we see as lines are three parallel poetic units that expand one whole meaning, as Hebrew poetry often does. The meaning grows right before our eyes, in these living and active words. In these three lines, various emphases emerge and surround that word "created" which appears in each line and threads them together.

The first line emphasizes "God created." He did it. That's the foundational fact. The second line repeats and emphasizes "in the image of God." In the NIV translation, this second line ends with the pronoun "them," which suggests already that this mankind, made in God's image, involves more than one person. The ESV, in the tradition of the King James version, reads, "In the image of God he created *him*" (my emphasis). Scholars disagree on the most faithful translation here. In either case, the third line completely and climactically unfolds the meaning: the mankind God created in his image consists of "male and female."

Another division or distinction is being made, which after the pattern of divisions and distinctions throughout the chapter should not surprise us. In the process of these three lines, the "mankind" (NIV) or "man" (ESV) grows clearer and separates into two distinct forms: male and female. Through this logically-connected process, we are being shown that, in our creation as male and female, we human beings reflect the image of God. As God calls himself "us," implying an internally relational nature, so we humans as male and female show the image of God in us as we relate both to him and to one another in all kinds of ways, in the process of ruling together over creation.

The rest of the Bible (and this book) unpacks what this process looks like, as men and women together work to create and sustain life in social units built on families with husbands and wives, fathers and mothers, sons and daughters. The ultimate unpacking will happen in the church family, as the New Testament shows us. But even in the very next chapter of Genesis we will glimpse more of what this joint rule looks like. The primary and foundational point here is that humanity's rule, showing forth God's image, involves the interaction of two distinct sexes: male and female. So the primary, foundational application here is that we should wholeheartedly embrace this distinction of the sexes as a good gift from God our Creator. It is not uncommon to hear people speak as if our creation as male and female is separate from and even secondary in importance to our creation in God's image. But as the Bible tells it, these truths are inseparable. Your gender (your identity as male or female) is a significant part of your creation as a human made in God's image.

God's speech to this first man and woman, even before telling them to subdue and rule, calls them to be fruitful and multiply and fill the earth (v 28). Of course, God had also called the living creatures to be fruitful and multiply— but without mentioning anything about their different sexes (v 22). Only for human beings is this engendered aspect of creation stated, and it is stated in the context of their bearing the very image of God. Although it clearly means that our physical bodies as God designed them are good, being made male and female involves more than just biological configuration or the ability to produce offspring. We humans are like the animals in many ways—made from the dust, made to reproduce—and yet we are different. We are made in the image of God.

God's Very Good Judgment

As Genesis 1 concludes, God blesses the first man and woman (v 28). He not only calls them to be fruitful and multiply, to subdue and rule; he also gives them for food "every plant yielding seed that is on the face of all the earth, and every tree with seed in its fruit" (v 29, ESV). God's first interactions with human beings are not heavy-handed or full of mean distinctions, but rather they are open-handed, overflowing with abundant provision from a good and generous Creator.

At last, as God finishes his creative work, we reach the overall judgment of God: "It was very good" (v 31). Here is the original judgment, by the Creator God, having completed the climactic step of creating male and female in his own likeness. This is the foundational pre-judgment to be made of all human beings: God's creation of us in his image, as male and female, is very good.

What does Genesis 1 show about human beings in relation to their Creator? It is clear that all humans, male and female, are equally created by God in his image. Humans are created to rule over creation together, showing their Creator's good rule. Our lives as male and female in relationship together are meant to show forth God's own image in us. Amazing. This sounds like a high calling, a very good one indeed. Nowhere else will a person find a greater dignity than in being created in the image of our Creator God. This is our human starting point, and we must never get over the wonder and the truth of it as we make our way through the Bible's unfolding story of God's dealings with his creation. It is the story with characters who are so valued by God that he made them in his own image, male and female. It is ultimately the story of a God so magnificent and so good that he created everything—and created male and female as the climax of it all, in his own image.

Receiving the Goodness of Gender

Genesis 1 (and the rest of the Scriptures) tells us that human gender is not an arbitrary, or self-determined, or socially-determined part of our identity; it is our identity as male or female according to God's good design of our biological sex. Voices in the media and in fact all around us urge us to let people discover and choose what gender they're most comfortable with, no matter what their biological sex. "Gender identity" has become a hugely volatile and politicized issue. Wikipedia, social media's engine of current and cooperative definitions, defines gender identity as "one's personal experience of one's own gender." Gender seems to have morphed into something defined by each person from the inside, rather than something gifted by a God who made and rules the universe.[4]

---

4 The issue of gender identity is large, and there is not space here to do justice to its nuances and its implications for the church. One helpful, biblical resource is Andrew Walker's *God and the Transgender Debate* (The Good Book Company, 2017). Rosaria Butterfield also helpfully discusses contemporary issues relating to gender and sexual identity, from a biblical and historical perspective. In *Openness Unhindered: Further Thoughts of an Unlikely Convert* (Crown & Covenant, 2015), she carefully (and beautifully) develops claims like the following: "By defining humanity according to sexual desires and segregating it according to its gendered object Freud was—intentionally or not—suppressing the biblical category of being made in God's image, male and female, and replacing it with the psychoanalytic category of sexual identity" (page 94).

One of the first and most evident facts we humans discover about a new baby is whether it is a boy or a girl.
There are indeed rare exceptions involving unusual combi-
nations of chromosomes or hormones or body parts that
make ambiguous the determination of sex; in those cases,
the immediate ambiguity about sex determination high-
lights the primacy of sex determination. Those experiencing the condition of "intersex" are, like all human beings,
fully made in the image of God, while suffering this particular effect of the fall (we'll reach the fall, and look at
its effects on the human race and our world, in chapter 3).
The point here is that when we cry out, "It's a boy!" or,
"It's a girl!" we are not imposing sexist, arbitrary, or au-
thoritarian distinctions on a human life; we are receiving
and celebrating the truth that this is how God made us, in
his image, male and female. It sounds radical these days to
affirm the Bible's teaching that male and female genders
were God's good idea, instituted as part of his sovereign
ordering of creation to show his own image in the people
he created. But the Bible's truth comes to us in the end not
like chains that bind us, but like a light that shows us the
path when we're flailing about in the dark, trying to find
our own way.

For a little girl who is struggling to figure out who she
is, how awesome and how ultimately compassionate it is
to teach her that she has a Creator who loves her, who
designed her female body purposefully and perfectly, and
who in fact intends for her to live out her femaleness in
a way that shows off her Creator. This doesn't mean she,
like the rest of us, won't struggle to walk in the light of
truth, as the next chapters in Genesis will explain. But it
means there is light, and that light is good. At a dinner
I recently attended, the topic of discussion was news of a
baby born whose parents refused to designate any sex on

the baby's birth certificate, so that the child would have the opportunity to grow up and choose a gender identity. Those parents were aiming to show compassion for that child, according to the wisdom of the world around us. According to the light of God's word, the most compassionate thing in the world would be to celebrate that child's creation as male or female.

We do not live in the kind of world described by Genesis 1, nor in the culture that existed when these words were first written down. But we can know that God intends humanity to continue living according to his creation order, no matter what our time and place in history. Jesus obviously thought so. During his earthly ministry Jesus was asked a question about divorce. He began his answer by referring to Genesis 1 v 27, making clear that this word from the beginning was normative for all people in all times: "Haven't you read ... that at the beginning the Creator 'made them male and female'?" (Matthew 19 v 4; see also Mark 10 v 6-9). If we don't start here, "at the beginning," in Genesis, we won't know how we got where we are—and we for sure won't be able to find our way forward.

The next chapter of Genesis will tell us a lot more about this first man and woman, and we'll continue to ask (even harder) questions about the way God makes distinctions between them. But it's crucial first to see this pair standing here before God in Genesis 1, made in his image, receiving his blessing, and hearing his voice together, equal and distinct. None of the unfolding of distinctions between them that will follow, in any part of the Bible, will contradict this foundational revelation of the equal value and glory of men and women made in the image of their Creator God. Even as we rightly oppose and strive to overcome a multitude of old prejudices, here is the most ancient and wonderful one—God's judgment from the beginning that his creation, including us as men and women made in our Creator's image, is very good. We can and must forever share God's "prejudice" that to be a woman, as to be a man, is very good.

Second Place?

I absolutely hate it when I come in toward the end of a really good conversation. Sometimes in holiday seasons when our extended family is gathered, I wake up at a reasonably early hour and come down for coffee to find my husband and children have all been up with the grandchildren since 5:00am, covering a whole world of discussion before the sun and I are even up. I can't ask them to rehearse it all again. I just wasn't there!

Or have you, like me, had the experience of getting the time wrong for a luncheon and arriving to find the introductions, appetizers, and first course over and done with? You can't ask them to do it all again. You've missed out.

Sometimes I feel like that for Eve when I read Genesis 2, because for the first half of it she's just not there. Think about what Eve misses. She's not there when God shapes the first man from the dust of the ground and breathes into his nostrils the breath of life (2 v 7). She misses the first breathtaking view of the garden planted by the Lord God himself—this lush garden filled with all these different kinds of trees pleasing to the eye and good for food, with the tree of life and the tree of the knowledge of good and evil at the center, and the river watering the garden and flowing out of it into four intricately described rivers… the words paint a fascinating picture!

But the woman is not yet in this picture; it is the man whom God first puts in the garden to work it and take care of it. Most dramatically, Eve misses hearing the voice of God in this scene, as he speaks directly and only to the man, telling him he's free to eat from any tree in the garden except one, the tree of the knowledge of good and evil: "for when you eat from it you will certainly die" (2 v 17).

Eve misses out on all these things. In Genesis 1 the man and woman appeared together, equally made in God's image and called to exercise dominion over creation. Now we're seeing that God made the man first and added the woman later. Why?

The Question of Order

Genesis 1 gives the cosmic overview. Genesis 2 zooms in and gives the close-up version, with characters front and center. Even God appears a little closer up. In chapter 1 we saw the sovereign Creator "God" (Hebrew *Elohim*); Genesis 2 introduces the name "LORD" (Hebrew *Yahweh*, the more personal name, expressing God's covenant love for his people).

We might have expected this chapter of Genesis to zoom in and show the first family together from the start. We might wonder why God didn't just form a man and a woman from the ground, show them around, and give them both that all-important command. Of the many questions we could ask of this chapter, we'll focus on this one: why did God create Adam first, and Eve second?

Many throughout history have suggested that the man was created first because he is qualitatively superior in some way to the woman. Even among venerable Church

Fathers one can trace such thinking.[5] Augustine of Hippo, back in the 4th century, wrote that:

> *"The woman together with her own husband is the image of God, so that that whole substance may be one image; but when she is referred separately to her quality of help-meet, which regards the woman herself alone, then she is not the image of God; but as regards the man alone, he is the image of God as fully and completely as when the woman too is joined with him in one."* [6]

Of course these words were written in a larger context, but it is clear that this Church Father, at least for the purposes of this passage, presented women as limited in the way they bear the image of God—in comparison to the way men do.

In the process of seeking to explain the apostle Paul's teaching on women, Augustine refers to Genesis 2, where the woman is created after the man to be a "help-meet" for him. This is what we need to talk about. How these first couple of chapters of the Bible go together is at the heart of our question. How does Genesis 2 follow Genesis 1 without negating any of chapter 1's meaning and power?

These are not just abstract questions about how to read a text. In the church, as in the wider world, a lot of hurt has been woven into the historical strands of thinking in

---

5 Although isolated examples need to be fleshed out in the context of a writer's work and thought, it's not hard to find them. The Church Father John Chrysostom, for example, wrote of the male sex enjoying "higher honor" and "superiority" over females, evidenced by being formed first. (See his *Homilies on Galatians, Ephesians, Philippians, Colossians, Thessalonians, Timothy, Titus, and Philemon*, translated Philip Schaff, Homily IX. ccel.org/ccel/schaff/npnf113.v.iii.x.html. Accessed 9/26/2017.)

6 *On the Holy Trinity*, translated Arthur West Haddan, Rev. William G. T. Shedd, from *The Complete Works of Saint Augustine*, ed. Philip Schaff (Kindle edition, 2013). Location 111592 of 216397.

regard to women. Maybe you have experienced the pain of being demeaned or harmed either in words or actions; maybe you have seen people demeaning or hurting women while claiming some sort of biblical warrant for doing so. This issue of how God regards women is not just theoretical; it is weighty, personal, and emotional.

Time for full confession: I don't completely understand why God chose to create Adam and Eve in the order he did. If there's anything we saw about God in Genesis 1, it's that he is distinct from and sovereign over his creation. His thoughts and his ways are higher than mine or yours. I will suggest two initial answers, not as a defense of the word but as an effort to receive and celebrate it fully. I love this word and this Lord who speaks it. Sometimes I chafe against it. But the more we look into it, the more we see its beauty.

Human Need and God's Provision

Here's the first reason we can discern from the Scriptures why Adam was created first: God was revealing both the man's great need and God's great gift to meet that need. Remember that we arrive in chapter 2 with that repeated divine verdict of Genesis 1 echoing in our minds: "Good"... "good"... "good"... "very good." So Genesis 2 v 18 brings us up short: God says, "It is not good." What is not good? "For the man to be alone."

This lack does not surprise the God of the universe; he could have avoided this problem from the beginning. But maybe God wanted Adam (and us) to sense deeply this aloneness, so that he (and we) could deeply savor the divine solution to it. That divine solution, which God declares he will make, is "a helper suitable for him" (v 18)—literally "a help as opposite him" or "a help corresponding to him."[7]

---

7   See Derek Kidner, *Genesis* in the Tyndale Old Testament Commentaries (IVP

God does not immediately do what he says he will do. First comes the naming ceremony of all the animals and all the birds; God brings them in procession before Adam "to see what he would name them" (v 19). It must have been an utterly pleasurable experience to relish the unique features and colors and textures and habits of these creatures with which God had filled the earth and sky, and to shape just the right name for each one—think of coming up with all those new words out of the creativity of a new, unfallen imagination!

But the woman isn't there yet. When she arrives, she will learn the animals' names just like Adam learned the names of day and night and seas and land and sky—and everything else God taught him about what had already been done when he came on the scene. God seems to be not only letting Adam's aloneness grow toward a dramatic resolution, but also teaching Adam about his place in this world, before making the woman who will help him in the work of ruling over it. He will be a better-equipped person for her to help, by the time she appears. In the meantime, he remains alone. In the animal-naming process, no suitable helper is found.

I wonder how much Adam did and did not understand about his aloneness. Surely he sensed it, and we will see his delight at the resolution of it. Surely we sense his need as we imagine the animals parading by with no suitable helper found. Through his word, God is revealing this need to us. But at this point the narrative does not take the turn we readers today might expect, with our bent toward psychological analysis; it actually pays no attention to Adam's personal perspective or feelings. The text doesn't say he felt alone; it says God judged that his being alone was not good. The text doesn't say Adam couldn't find a suitable helper among the animals; it says one was not found. God is the one driving the story as he brings all the creatures to the man to see what he will name them. After all, Adam would not know how to look for or find this helper, or even how to imagine her.

This narrative lights up God's desire on behalf of his creation for it to be complete—for the man to have a life that is only "good." We readers might instinctively focus just on Adam's experience—and we're invited to do that before long. But this story is ultimately about God and his care toward us his creatures. The point is that he's out for our good. The woman is not missing or missing out in this story; the woman is the crucial final link in this story through which God shows himself to us.

In the order of creation of the man and the woman, God is revealing Adam's great need, and God's correspondingly great provision to meet that need. God sees and cares that the man is alone, and God acts to solve his aloneness. God prepares him for the answer to his aloneness. That's what God is like. Ultimately, the Scriptures will tell us of how God acted to solve humanity's greatest need and remove our eternal aloneness, fully and finally, through his own Son.

Provision of a Suitable Helper

So God takes a rib from the sleeping man and "the rib that the LORD God had taken from the man he made into a woman" (v 22, ESV). Who could have imagined that God would make a woman from one of the man's ribs? God brings her to the man, just like he brought the animals to him, and the man names her, just like he named the animals—but this is completely different! We're suddenly looking at two persons, two that are alike (of the same flesh) and yet not identical; the woman is "corresponding" to, or perfectly "suitable" for, him. And now we get the man's perspective. He celebrates with a poem! In this first recorded human speech, notice the poetic lines that match and balance against each other. These lines have the same beautiful symmetry experienced in the meeting of this first perfectly-matched man and woman:

> *This is now bone of my bones*
> *and flesh of my flesh;*
> *she shall be called "woman,"*
> *for she was taken out of man. (Genesis 2 v 23)*

The words used here for "woman" and "man" look and sound alike in the Hebrew (*issa* and *is*). He was one; now they are two; but the chapter's concluding words show that as husband and wife they come together again, as "one flesh" (v 24). Perfectly matched. No coverings or separations. No shame in the full sharing of one's self with the other. Adam's aloneness has been ended by God in the amazing provision of a suitable helper, a wife.

God in his goodness created this first husband and wife to be perfectly suited for sexual intimacy. Verse 24 is God's pronouncement on the matter based on the pattern established in this first union: God is saying that this is good. We saw in the previous chapter that, as Jesus began to answer a question about divorce, he quoted Genesis 1 v 27, affirming God's creation of male and female (Matthew 19 v 4). In that same answer Jesus goes right on to quote Genesis 2 v 24 (Matthew 19 v 5), affirming the lasting goodness of marriage between a man and woman, using God's words from that first wedding ceremony.

Suitable, Yes, But *Helper*?

But what about that word "helper" (Genesis 2 v 18)? Even as we keep all our good "prejudices" set in place by Genesis 1, remembering that the man and woman are equally made in the image of God, we still might wonder: doesn't the word "helper" applied to the woman imply she's some sort of second-class citizen (in a society of two!)? When we think of a "helper," we commonly think of a household helper, or a child who is "Mommy's little helper," or any number of roles of seemingly lesser importance or responsibility.

But let's think about the word itself. A helper is simply someone who brings aid to someone else. To help does not demean the helper. In fact, quite the contrary. On several occasions recently I've been helpless to communicate in a foreign country—and the translators who helped me were heroes in my eyes. I was amazed and humbled by their expertise in maneuvering from one language to another. I was the one lacking, not them. And when I was in need, their help rescued me!

The word helper (Hebrew *ezer*) is a word denoting strength—often the kind of strength that wins battles. In fact, throughout the Old Testament this word is often used to describe God, as he helps his people— "The LORD is with me; he is my helper" (Psalm 118 v 7). The helper given to Adam is an extension of God's own help to him, as God himself makes the woman and brings her to him. The helper is God's means of turning "not good" into "very good." The helper is the high point, the climactic completion of God's creation story. The helper role of woman is a high calling: one through which she reflects the image of God her Creator—and through which she serves God as she walks according to his word.

Still, we must ask what it means in practice to say that

woman is a "helper suitable for him." In Genesis 2, this
high helper role clearly applies to this first marriage (and to
all subsequent ones, as we shall see more and more clearly). But does it apply to all women in all their relations with
all men? Are all women to be helpers of all men? Is the
"helper" nature intrinsic to womanhood, according to God's
plan? If by saying yes to that question we think of "helper"
in any dismissive or demeaning way, then the answer is no.
There's no teaching in Scripture that would lead us there.

If by saying yes to that question we confuse biblically-
defined roles with other roles, then the answer is no. We
will come to passages that deal with roles both in marriage and in the church, and Scripture is clear about both
contexts. The Bible's teaching in both contexts reaches
back to Genesis for its foundational truth. But if we apply
Scripture's teaching about these roles in contexts to which
God's word does not speak, then we can get into trouble.
I'm going to claim in a moment that this creation story
does let us glimpse a creational and universal pattern that
applies to all men and all women, so that there is a sense in
which all women are called to be "helpers." But if I should
take that universal pattern to mean, for example, that a
woman should not lead a business, or be president of a
college, or a country, then I would be confusing biblically-
defined roles with other roles to which Scripture does not
speak. I would be putting unbiblical restrictions on God's
female image-bearers.

But we can say yes to that question in a way that maintains the "good prejudices" of Genesis 1, and at the same
time asserts that this first male and female teach us something deep and universal. Just as Genesis reveals the foundational truth that male and female (not just husbands and
wives) are created in God's image, so it would seem there
is foundational truth in the creation of the first woman

(not just the first wife) as a helper to the man. It's hard to pin down this truth to specific principles, because the truth of what happens in creation grows and spreads its light throughout Scripture. We'll need to get to the context of the church to find the full and open working out of these creational truths among the body of brothers and sisters (married or single) within the family of God. It's in the context of local church congregations that I have most vividly witnessed the beauty of partnership between women who actively help all those around them and men who welcome and appreciate that help, as God's people serve and work together.

There's a single woman in my home congregation who is brilliant in financial matters, and everybody celebrates her brilliance; I don't know what we would do without her help, which she has given for years unreservedly to the church—eventually as a staff member. She is a woman who respects, celebrates, and helps the men in leadership. The high helper role of women, when women take it to heart, tends to flavor everything they do, within and without the church. This woman was treasured in the bank where she for years held a position of great responsibility. I imagine you can think of women who flavor your life and your church with a helping spirit, and men who delight to partner with such women, humbly receiving their help no matter who is in charge, in any kind of work or enterprise. We'll talk more and more specifically about these applications. In fact, more light will come from this next reason we find for God's creation order.

Order in Humanity

The first reason for the order of the creation of man and woman was to show the man's great need, and God's great gift to meet that need. We can discern a second reason: God means to establish order in humanity. That's a controversial statement. But it actually makes sense if we remember the ordered pattern of creation all through Genesis 1: God has authoritatively made divisions and distinctions, handed out responsibilities, and delegated dominion, all because he is the good and sovereign God. The sun and the moon are to rule over the day and the night, respectively and not interchangeably. The man and woman together are to rule over the fish and birds and animals. When we zoom in further, then, it might not completely surprise us that there is some order even between the man and the woman, who are equally created in the image of God.

The intentionality of God's order in creation's first five days prepares us to find significance in the order of the sixth day. This order has ramifications. The first created human being, the man, first receives God's word; he then bears a responsibility for receiving it, keeping it, and passing it on. It is the man whom God first places in the garden to care for it; he is the first steward of creation. It is the man to whom God explains the freedom to eat from any tree, along with the command not to eat of the tree of the knowledge of good and evil, and the result of disobeying that command.

We see the man walking ahead and alone into a number of responsibilities. God calls the man to name the animals, thereby exercising human dominion over them as he displays the image of God, whom we've just seen naming what he makes. Interestingly, it is the man who God says initiates the leaving of father and mother to become united to his wife—not the other way round. Just as the sun and moon are not interchangeable, so the man and woman are not interchangeable. The man is given the instructions and put to work, and the woman then joins him as his helper.

This does not mean they don't work together. This does not mean we give up our Genesis 1 "prejudices." This does mean that Adam is not made to be Eve's helper—Eve is made to be Adam's. He bears the responsibility of leading Eve in all that he has been given to know and do before she arrived on the scene. This makes sense: to lead means to go out before, so that others follow. Eve cannot bear that leadership responsibility because she wasn't there before. According to the order in which God has acted, she bears the responsibility of hearing and following all Adam tells her of what he has experienced and learned. We have seen them together receiving God's blessing and God's call to be fruitful and fill the earth and subdue it. They are partners, and Adam appears to be the partner who leads.

If you're like me, you might instinctively chafe against this order. You may accept it as true, because the Bible teaches it—but how can you or I celebrate it as good? This struggle arises partly because we tend to associate difference in roles with difference in value. As soon as we bring up the word "leader" in reference to a man, and "helper" in reference to a woman, assumptions begin to fly—assumptions that if a man is in leadership, he is more important, and that if a woman is not in leadership but "merely" a helper, she is less important.

Why do we assume that a difference in role makes a difference in value? We can't really deal with that question without going on to Genesis 3. But if what we've observed in Genesis 1 and 2 is accurate, then we can at least affirm, even if we don't completely understand it, that the ordered relationship of the first man and woman was very good. There is no question about lack of value or importance in these beginning scenes. The whole progression of creation, from the planets to the people, is presented as a wonder-worthy work of God! We see only joy in the coming together of the first man and woman, created in God's image to reflect him and obey him as the beautiful climax of the creation order.

Further, logically speaking, which one of us would really want to equate role with human value? We surely wouldn't want to say that a wealthy CEO is more valuable than someone who is disabled and out of work, or that a beautiful film star in her twenties is more valuable than an elderly woman or a newborn baby. Even though we often live in a way that assigns value according to roles, deep down we humans know better. Deep down, we often long for our value not to be linked to roles we play or positions we hold, but to something beyond these things. And that longing is met in the truths of Genesis 1 and 2—in the revelation that our Creator has made us in his image, male and female together. It's only in his eyes that ultimate value is measured.

It's certainly counter-cultural, but this truth about ordered distinctions is in fact a good gift of revelation from God. It adjusts our eyesight to focus on him, and to find our value ultimately in him. As we peer into the beginnings of the human story, we see a Creator who establishes an order that actually reflects himself and that shows his full goodness in every part of that order.

As you read this, the sun is declaring God's glory, still carrying out its original assignment, rising at daybreak all around the earth like a bridegroom coming out of his chamber (Psalm 19 v 1-6). Likewise, all men and women can show God's glory in the ordered relationships of our lives together. Genesis gives the crucial foundation. We'll get into more of the practical entailments later. We'll wrestle in subsequent chapters with the Old Testament laws regarding women, and with the New Testament's teaching on marriage and the church. But we had to start here, and we need to keep remembering the God we see here; this same good God—Father, Son, and Holy Spirit—is revealing himself from beginning to end.

We're about to ask more questions—hard ones—about the first woman (and all the women who come after). As we ask, our hope and our help is that in the Bible's God-breathed words, God actually shows himself to us. His word can bear the weight of our questions.

Fallen Women

G enesis 3 is one of the most well-known chapters in
the entire Bible—largely because of the woman in the
story, Eve. To many, it seems like Eve is given an exception-
ally hard time, on both the front and back end of this story. As we look at it, we'll need to ask some hard questions
about how God treats his first female image-bearer.

The Fall

Genesis 3 has two main parts: the story of the fall, and
the fallout from the fall. Maybe the most surprising thing
as the curtain opens is that God is not there—at least not
openly. He's been the main actor on the Genesis stage so
far, pervasively present as he's directed the process of
creation, right through the union of the first man and
woman. That's where we left off at the end of Genesis 2—
Adam and Eve together, naked and without shame, ready
to enjoy living as God's image-bearers and ruling as his
representatives in his creation.

But out of the shadows emerges the serpent. God is not
on the stage, but suddenly in verse 1 this serpent *is*: "Now
the serpent was more crafty than any of the wild animals

the LORD God had made." He's there, he's probably beautiful—and he talks. Separated from its "kind" of wild animals over whom humankind is to rule, this crafty creature is clearly out of order. I think we're meant to think (and surely Eve thought), "What's a serpent doing speaking?" But we hardly have time to think, because, as the serpent speaks, he immediately insinuates himself between one of the human beings and God.

The rest of Scripture helps us identify this serpent as Satan, who is mentioned in the book of Revelation as "that ancient serpent called the devil, or Satan, who leads the whole world astray" (Revelation 12 v 9; 20 v 2). It appears that Satan entered and spoke through this creature, aiming to lead Eve astray. Watch the progression of questioning, adding to, and finally directly contradicting God's word:

> *He said to the woman, "Did God really say, 'You must not eat from any tree in the garden'?"*
>
> *The woman said to the serpent, "We may eat fruit from the trees in the garden, but God did say, 'You must not eat fruit from the tree that is in the middle of the garden, and you must not touch it, or you will die.'"*
>
> *"You will not certainly die," the serpent said to the woman. "For God knows that when you eat from it your eyes will be opened, and you will be like God, knowing good and evil." (Genesis 3 v 1b-5)*

And Eve falls for it. She's tempted in three ways: the fruit of the tree is good for food, pleasing to the eye, and desirable for gaining wisdom (v 6). Not only her physical senses are aroused, but also a desire to raise herself up to God's level rather than submit herself to God's word.

Abruptly comes the moment of tragedy: "She took some and ate it." Just a little phrase tells of such a deep fall.

Once Eve is taken in, the rest of the action rushes by. The next brief sentence, somewhat casual-sounding, carries an electric shock: "she also gave some to her husband, who was with her, and he ate it." Reading those words, we experience the kind of super-accelerated thought process that flashes through our minds at the height of a crisis.

Ah, so he's there with her?

And he's done nothing?

He didn't step in to defend God's word, which he heard with his own ears?

He just watched Eve eat?

He's eating it too?

And it's over, like a tornado really, which suddenly and quickly points its finger of destruction at one spot and then moves on, leaving devastation behind.

What the sin leaves behind is shame. In contrast to the "no shame" of the last chapter, now "the eyes of both of them were opened, and they realized they were naked; so they sewed fig leaves together and made coverings for themselves" (v 7). Trust has dissolved and openness has disappeared. They may already be fighting between themselves about what just happened. Sin has invaded and begun to break apart the order of God's good creation.

Portraits of Eve

Why did the serpent target Eve and not Adam? Being crafty, he evidently figured out that this would work—but why? Well, we're not told. From his success, we can see both that Eve was vulnerable to the draw of the serpent and that Adam was vulnerable to the draw of… Eve. Eve is the central human character in this drama; no wonder that, for centuries, people have felt compelled to try to explain her.

Some conclude that Eve was simply not as smart as Adam. She was dull. That's why the serpent could so easily wind her into his cunning logic, whereas Adam (so the thinking goes) would have figured him out and told him to get lost. The apostle Paul distinguishes between Adam and Eve in their processing of the temptation: "Adam was not the one deceived; it was the woman who was deceived and became a sinner" (1 Timothy 2 v 14). Does this mean Adam was smarter than Eve?

Others have taken Eve to be not less smart, but more evil. She was drawn to the devil even in the midst of a perfect life in a beautiful garden with a loving husband and the very presence of God—how could she? How evil! The third-century writer Tertullian authored a book, *On the Apparel of Women*, in which he reminds all women that they share Eve's "ignominy ... of original sin and the odium of being the cause of the fall of the human race":

> *"Do you not know that you are [each] an Eve? The sentence of God on this sex of yours lives in this age: the guilt must of necessity live too. You are the devil's gateway: you are the unsealer of that [forbidden] tree: you are the first deserter of the divine law: you are she who persuaded him whom the devil was not valiant enough to attack. You destroyed so easily God's image, man. On account of your desert—that is, death—even the Son of God had to die."* [8]

Let's add one more portrait to go alongside "dull Eve"

8 *On the Apparel of Women*, Book I, chapter 1, translated S. Thelwall. From *Ante-Nicene Fathers*, Volume IV, ed. Philip Schaff. bit.ly/2fnZR7F; accessed 9/26/2017.

and "evil Eve": that of "sexual-temptress Eve." Many early artists' portrayals of Eve presented her in alluring positions, holding out that fruit while offering obviously much more than the fruit. In such a scenario, poor Adam comes off as helpless under the power of Eve's sexual advances. Eve becomes the archetypal *femme fatale*—paving the way, reads the implicit message, for all females after her.

The whole of Genesis 3 will help us grapple with these portraits, but let's make a start. Was Eve less intelligent than Adam and so an easier target? The Bible gives no evidence of this. Eve actually seems quite articulate—certainly more so than Adam in this scene! Although the Bible says she was "deceived," it wasn't inability to reason that caught her up; it was desire—the fruit was *good* and *pleasing* and *desirable*. Actually, we might ascribe Eve's vulnerability to Adam's lack of diligence in leading her well. We must remember it was he to whom God originally gave the command not to eat of this fruit. Why did he not LEAP into that conversation, declare God's word, and rescue Eve from deception?

Adam's wrong does not cancel out Eve's—but it was no less wrong. Ultimately, the vulnerability of both Adam and Eve was their vulnerability to temptation and sin. So in Genesis 3, Eve is not presented as more evil than Adam. They both fell, one right after the other. The issue of order is crucial, and Paul addresses it when he talks about Eve's sin. Right before his comment about Eve's being deceived, Paul writes, "For Adam was formed first, then Eve" (1 Timothy 2 v 13). Why does Paul point to this order? Because Adam had a primary responsibility in that scene back in Eden. And he didn't step up to it. We'll see God's view of this in the next verses.

As to the charge that Eve used her sexual wiles to entice Adam to eat the fruit, I suppose it's possible. But there's no scriptural support for this view. Adam was certainly not helpless: "He ate it." He did it. You might say that's the climax of the action here. Adam wasn't helpless, and he wasn't deceived; he knew exactly what the voice of God had said, but he listened to the voice of his wife and chose to disobey.

In Genesis 3 v 1-7 we witness not a female failure, but rather a human one. The woman may have opened the door to sin, but Adam could and should have closed it. The various portraits of Eve as dull or evil or temptress are unfair. But this Scripture isn't. And the God of Scripture isn't. Let's go on.

The Fallout

After the fall comes the fallout. The man and woman have both broken the word of their Creator, and their Creator comes and deals with them—and with the serpent. As we witness these interactions, at least two questions arise. First, *why does God approach Adam first, if it's Eve who sinned first?* Second, *how shall we deal with the severity of God's judgment addressed to the woman?*

It's a dramatic, mysterious moment when in verse 8 "the man and his wife" hear the sound of the Lord God "as he was walking in the garden in the cool of the day," and they hide among the trees. But God calls out to the man, "Where are you?" (v 9). God confronts Adam with his disobedience, at which point Adam steps up and owns it, admits his guilt, speaks up for his wife... No! He doesn't! "The woman you put here with me—she gave me some fruit from the tree, and I ate it" (v 12). He blames her. This is a low, low point for Adam. At the moment of temptation, Adam wasn't there for his wife. Now, in the presence of God, he's not only not there for her but he blames her, and blames God for making her.

The answer to why Adam must take first responsibility has to do with order. Think of what just happened: the serpent brought disorder to every part of creation, from the bottom up. All are displaced; the rightful relation is broken step by step between serpent and woman, woman and man, man and God. So now God addresses his creation in a re-ordered progression. It would be a comic sequence if it weren't tragic: God to the man, who blames the woman; God to the woman who blames the serpent; God to the serpent. His words to the serpent are a kind of pivot that begins his declarations of judgment, which turn and travel back along the same trail: serpent, woman, man. God addresses first and finally the man: Adam gets the first question (v 9) and the final judgment (v 17-19). God gives two reasons for that judgment: because Adam ate, and because "you listened to your wife" (v 17).

The emphasis on order is really the point. Though Eve sinned first, Adam was created first, received God's words first, and bore first and final responsibility to obey and to lead his wife in obeying those words. This order of responsibility doesn't take away responsibility on anyone's part. God doesn't let Eve off the hook: "What is this you have done?" he asks her (v 13). She, too, shifts the blame: "The serpent deceived me, and I ate." Everybody's blaming others here, and everybody is guilty.

The Painful Judgment

As we come to God's judgments, let's start with the middle one, addressed to the woman:

> *I will make your pains in childbearing very severe;*
> *with painful labor you will give birth to children.*

Your desire will be for your husband,
and he will rule over you. (v 16)

Reading this verse makes us almost blurt out our second question: *Is this fair?* It sounds so harsh. Part of the problem is that we know the painful-labor-in-childbearing part is no exaggeration; it's been proven oh-so-painfully by oh-so-many women. And then the husband-ruling-over part... how are we to understand that? Let's consider this challenging little verse, which carries such large implications for generations of women.

Looking at the first two lines about painful labor, we can't help but compare them to the judgment on the man that follows:

Cursed is the ground because of you;
through painful toil you will eat food from it
all the days of your life.
It will produce thorns and thistles for you,
and you will eat the plants of the field.
By the sweat of your brow you will eat your food...
(v 17-19a)

These judgments fit together, even as Adam and Eve were made to fit together. For both the man and the woman, God's words describe the ways in which his good created order will now become onerous. When it was embraced, God's order was harmonious. Now rejected, it becomes painful. The "pains in childbearing" and "painful labor" of the woman are matched by the "painful toil" the man will experience in producing food from the cursed and thorny ground. Both will suffer the consequences of sin in their efforts to follow God's original command to be fruitful and multiply, filling and subduing the earth (1 v 28).

It helps to see the symmetry. And yet... the pain of child-bearing seems heavy on the scales when we weigh these judgments against each another. Women sometimes smile when men complain about various ailments; men simply can't know what pain women routinely experience—not only in the agonizing pains of birthing a child, but also in all the associated pain of longing for children; of having bodies that keep reminding us we are equipped to bear children; of carrying children; of losing children from our own bodies—and of dying in childbirth, as so many women did in earlier centuries and still do, especially in places without access to medical help.

On the other hand, women don't fully know the pain many men experience when they try to provide for a family and find little success—whether in growing crops or companies. This is a tricky comparison, because men cannot bear children, but women can participate in the workplace. Many women have shared alongside men the frustrations of toiling, and have shed the sweat of their brows—whether in grinding the grain or making the clothes or keeping the books. Women actually seem to bear the brunt of not just one but both of these judgments!

But having seen Genesis' emphasis on ordered distinctions, and seeing the parallel judgment on women, we can reasonably conclude that the man's judgment here includes the distinct pain of the one who bears the responsibility to lead and provide for a family. This leadership can be exercised in all sorts of ways, and through various kinds of work. But it does mean a special weight of responsibility. I imagine that you, like me, know a number of men who carry the responsibility of their family heavy on their shoulders and who never seem to feel able to provide sufficiently, or securely. We probably often underestimate this ongoing pain. Interestingly, God's words about childbearing pain here in Genesis 3 are brief—they are intense and concentrated, like labor pains. The words to Adam about the pain of work stretch through extended lines, like the daily slogging through an unproductive job, or through unproductive efforts even to find one.

God gives the final and ultimate judgment to the man, declaring that he will return to the ground from which he was taken: "For dust you are, and to dust you will return" (3 v 19b). Here applied is the judgment of death explained first to Adam when God gave him the command not to eat of the tree of the knowledge of good and evil. This judgment spreads from Adam not only to Eve but to the entire human race. We'll come back to this.

Desire and Rule

But what of those last two lines of God's pronouncement to the woman: "Your desire will be for your husband, and he will rule over you" (v 16)? Again, how is this fair? Is God giving the man a warrant to rule over the woman, who simply desires him? We see conflict set up between *desire* and *rule*, as God here declares the results of sin—but we need to ask what these words mean. And we need to ask humbly, acknowledging that these are not easy words to understand.

These lines do not sound strange in the context of Genesis 3—we have just seen a pattern of conflict between the man and woman acted out for the first time. Each has aimed not good but harm against the other in a manner that directly contradicts her or his rightful role. Eve has not helped Adam follow God's word but has desired to draw him with her into sin: she not only ate the fruit, but gave it to him. And Adam not only hasn't led Eve according to God's word but also has used his position to treat her harshly, putting her down to defend himself before God. Now, according to this judgment, the pattern of sin they've each chosen will persist, hardening into ongoing mutual strife. In one sense this is exactly fair.

It helps to look not just back but also ahead in the text, to understand further this "desire" and "rule." In the very next chapter, God again puts these two words together when he tells Adam's and Eve's angry son, Cain, "Sin is crouching at your door; it desires to have you, but you must rule over it" (4 v 7).[9] Here the two words again communicate a power struggle involving sin, which sheds light backwards on the nature of the struggle in chapter 3. The repeated word pattern does not and need not lead to a one-to-one correspondence of the different characters involved in the two verses; this is a resonance of context, with both verses exposing the conflict brought about by the fall. There are differences; unlike 4 v 7, there is no warrant in 3 v 16 for such struggle, but rather, simply a declaration that this will be the continuing painful effect of sin. In general, then, the contexts immediately before and after 3 v 16 point to this desire and rule as two sides of a sin-soaked battle.

Other than Genesis 3 and 4, Scripture's only other use of this word "desire" comes in Song of Songs 7 v 10, where we hear a wife celebrating her husband's sexual desire for her: "His desire is for me," she says. How hugely encouraging is this Old Testament glimpse of the one-flesh-ness of marriage as God ordained it, and as it ultimately can be

---

9   In a 2016 update of the English Standard Version, Crossway's translation committee changed the word "for" in both Genesis 3 v 16 and Genesis 4 v 7 to the words "contrary to." ("Against" had previously been footnoted for both verses as an alternative translation.) Without entering the debate on translation theories involved in such decisions, I would agree that this change does clarify the meaning of Genesis 3 v 16, more specifically connecting the adversarial conflict in chapter 4 with that in chapter 3.

restored in Christ! But in light of Song of Songs, should we ask whether this word "desire" connotes longing, including sexual longing, back in Genesis 3 v 16? It's logically possible, especially since both contexts are that of marriage. The most powerful pointers, however, come from the clear, close Genesis contexts, which portray the pervasive ravages of sin at the heart of all—including the woman. In any case, what is abundantly and tragically clear in Genesis 3 v 16 is that desire will meet rule, resulting in a relationship of conflict due to sin.

Genesis 3 shows us the source and nature of our struggles as sinful women and men. No, not all women are manipulative, trying to control men to get what they desire. No, not all men are domineering, ruling with harshness over women. We should take utmost care not to judge one another's actions simply in light of these sinful patterns. But we must admit these patterns persist, even as God said they would. I could tell you and you could tell me of the struggles we've known and seen in the context of marriage, often relating to power tugs-of-war. I know I'm not the only one who has female friends whose husbands have "ruled" their wives harshly, or who has observed marriages in which a wife demeans her husband or uses him for her own desired, selfish ends.

It's not always big, dramatic struggles. I had a conversation just this morning with a couple I encountered on a sunny street corner. The man was impatient and kept interrupting his wife, telling her they needed to go. The woman kept interrupting back, ignoring him with rolls of her eyes while continuing to talk. It felt like being in the middle of a little war. I say that with empathy, because we've all, myself included, fought plenty of little wars.

Of course men and women struggle against each other in many of these same ways outside of marriage—including in the workplace, and in religious contexts. It's commonplace to hear about women and men vying for power, opportunity, and reward in these contexts. Sexual abuse of women happens in any number of contexts, as men use their power in order to rule over women and take from them what they want. And women learn ways of getting from men what they want, whether through appeal to a man's ego or to his physical or sexual appetite, or sometimes by simply taking advantage of a man's weak will. I don't doubt you can think of painful examples in your world, and maybe even in your own home or heart. Genesis is full of them. Read a few more pages and you'll soon come upon Abraham, who made his wife Sarah pretend to be his sister in order to protect himself, and let her be taken by an Egyptian Pharaoh into his palace. Of course it's Sarah who made Abraham sleep with her maid, because she wanted that son…

According to the Bible we've inherited these human family traits from our first mother and father. The selfishness of sin has invaded all of our hearts. Genesis 3 is neither a mandate nor an excuse for these traits; it shows the origin of this fallen world and the reality of the pain that we, along with Adam and Eve, have chosen in rejecting the word of the Creator.

The Seed of Hope

We skipped God's words to the serpent. Let's go back there now, because those words carry the seed of hope at the center of this devastating chapter of Genesis. After cursing the serpent, God adds a promise:

> *I will put enmity*
> *between you and the woman,*
> *and between your offspring and hers;*

> *he will crush your head,*
>   *and you will strike his heel. (3 v 15)*

Many call this declaration the *protoevangelium*—the first gospel announcement. God promises that an offspring of the woman will crush the head of this serpent—that is, deal the serpent a mortal blow. The serpent will strike the heel of that offspring, or seed—he will wound him, but not destroy him. And so is spoken the first promise of the Savior, the Lord Jesus Christ. Here is the seed of hope, the only hope for us fallen human beings: the gospel.

In explaining the gospel, Paul looks back to Genesis and turns to Adam as the human representative, the one carrying original responsibility for sin and death. Paul draws a line between two men, Adam and Christ: "For since death came through a man, the resurrection of the dead comes also through a man. For as in Adam all die, so in Christ all will be made alive" (1 Corinthians 15 v 21-22). How does Christ bring life where Adam brought death? Christ was born into the human race, lived a sinless life, and died on the cross bearing our sins: he gave himself to be struck in the heel by that serpent Satan. But then he rose from the dead—and that resurrection was the death-blow of Satan. When we put our faith in Christ, who was the promised seed, we receive eternal life that replaces the eternal death we had in Adam.

The first man seems to grasp the hope of the man to come: "Adam named his wife Eve, because she would become the mother of all the living" (Genesis 3 v 20). He's heard. He's already looking for the promised offspring. The hope shines out: Eve has received not only the judgment that women will suffer pain in childbearing, but also the promise of a child to be born who will end all pain. All women—and all humans—can hear that promise along with Eve. All of us can receive the certain hope of the gospel.

The hope of the gospel is a hope that first of all acknowledges human sin. Genesis 3 is clear that Eve and Adam both disobeyed God's command. Although Adam is held responsible before God and throughout salvation history, Eve is no less and no more sinful than her husband. Women don't have to bear the burden of being thought better, or thought worse, than men; we humans together live out the devastating consequences of the fall. How freeing to acknowledge our sin, to see the world as it really is, and to bow in repentance before God, claiming his mercy and his promise of salvation in Christ.

The hope of the gospel overflows with mercy—which means we fallen human beings are spared the punishment our sin deserves. Our merciful Creator did not let the story of the human race end in the Garden of Eden. The Creator and Judge is also the God of our salvation, the one who promised that seed. As Genesis 3 comes to a close, we see a merciful Creator who knows his fallen creatures' shame and need for covering: "The LORD God made garments of skin for Adam and his wife and clothed them" (v 21). Imagine those moments of being dressed by God. The chapter ends with evident mercy, as God shuts the man and woman out of Eden so that they will not eat from the tree of life and live forever in their sin.

The hope of the gospel is finally a hope that lies in God himself. We humans—we males and females—are not the hope of the world. We are not good in ourselves. No human solution or emancipation will address the depths of our fall. Only God, our sovereign Creator and our righteous Judge, is able to conquer sin and death, restore our relationship with himself and one another, and make his fallen creation new. The beautiful truth is that in Genesis 3, amid the wreckage caused by the sin of both humans, God promised an offspring who would accomplish all that. In Christ, it was accomplished. On this foundation, we can read on with hope, even as we move through some of the hardest parts of the human story.

The Darkest Places

"When you go to war against your enemies and the LORD your God delivers them into your hands and you take captives, if you notice among the captives a beautiful woman and are attracted to her, you may take her as your wife" (Deuteronomy 21 v 10-11).

What?

Many readers might find it tempting just to stop there and conclude that whoever the God of this book is, we don't want him. Or, if we want the God of the Bible, we don't want the God of *this* part.

Our family once lived in a house where there were dark closed-off parts I never entered—and they haunted me sometimes. There was an extensive crawl space under the house that various workers entered with flashlights from time to time, to investigate leaks or rodents. In the room over the garage there were a couple of little doors cut into the paneling that, when forced, would open into shadowy spaces hidden above the garage ceiling. I peeked, but never in a decade did I open wide those doors to see what was really there. I think I was afraid of coming face to face with a rodent of some kind—maybe a big, scary one.

For a lot of us, parts of the Old Testament are like those

dark, unexplored places—and we're afraid, perhaps based on a conversation or a book or a half-forgotten confusion when we sought to read through the Bible years ago, that there may be bad things there. At the heart of such fears often lurks a vague and shadowy image of God that we've created for ourselves, out of our fears. And those fears lead us to doubt that God is good. Specifically, when we hear about some of these passages concerning women, we are susceptible to voices whispering in our ears that God is not good to women.

As we explore some of these passages, a scary creature does confront us—but it's human, not divine. It's our human self, in our fallen condition. One of the most important parts of digging into Old Testament stories is our inevitable encounter with the depths of sin and its effects on the human race.

This is hard. We so want to believe that the people around us are good. From a woman's perspective I know this well: a daughter desperately wants to trust her dad, to see him as her wise and strong protector—sometimes despite evidence to the contrary. A wife wants to believe that her husband has a good heart and would never ever harm her—but very likely you, like me, have known even seemingly upright church elders who have utterly surprised their families and churches, leaving everything behind for other relationships, rejecting outright the authority of God's word. Perhaps you, like me, have spoken with women who love the men in their lives, but who are frightened by those men's dark tendencies toward too much alcohol, or pornography, or violent anger. Many women are afraid of what lurks in these dark places, and of exposing their loved ones by talking about it—which is why so many never do. Men also have deep fears, in regard to women; I just don't know their fears as well. Of course at bottom are fears about the dark places that lurk inside ourselves.

The worst trouble comes when we turn these fears toward God himself. One of the books from which I will quote is titled *Is God a Moral Monster? Making Sense of the Old Testament God.*[10] Questions like that one arise partly because we do not explore the depths of God's word and so we do not come to know him well. We can easily create a dark god in the image of human beings, rather than trusting the God of light, who created us. There is a reason why many pagan cultures have imagined gods that demand the sexual abuse of girls and women as part of religious rituals; they have made gods in their own images rather than seeking the God in whose image they are made.

Only God is good, and God is only good—never evil. If we will listen, the Bible will tell us so. It will tell us so even as we visit Old Testament passages that are full of human evil. The Bible's message is worse than we like to think, in regard to our sin; but it is much better than we dream, in regard to our hope. We'll find both extremes as we explore first some dark places in the Old Testament law, and then a dark period of Old Testament history.

Dark Places in the Law

In the book of Deuteronomy, Moses, at the end of his life, is addressing a new generation of Israelites who have grown up in the wilderness and who are finally ready to enter the land God promised. These are the descendants of Abraham, whose offspring God promised to multiply and bless, and through whom God would bless all the

---

10 This book, by Paul Copan (Baker, 2011), is a helpful discussion of some of the common and most challenging ethical questions stimulated by various Old Testament texts.

nations of the world (Genesis 12 v 1-7). The covenant agreement with Abraham further unfolded that *protoevangelium* promise given in Eden: God chose Abraham's seed to channel that promise. He multiplied them, delivered them from slavery in Egypt, and gave them his law as they gathered at Mount Sinai in the wilderness. Despite their repeated disobedience to that law, God preserved and provided for them. Now, on the brink of the promised land, Moses preaches the law to them, calling them to listen to their Lord, love him, and obey him with all their hearts.

In this "Mosaic law" comes not only the unchanging moral foundation of the Ten Commandments but also the laws that applied specifically to the Israelites in that time and place. For example, there were "ceremonial laws"—all about burnt sacrifices and worship practices—which are no longer binding on God's people today, because Jesus fulfilled them when he came and offered the perfect, final sacrifice for sin, on the cross (Hebrews 10 v 11-14). There were also many "case laws": these laws applied the moral principles of the Ten Commandments to particular issues ("cases") faced by Israel as a nation back then—issues often not faced by believers today. We Christians don't live now as a nation but as a people united in Christ, scattered among the nations. In the course of salvation history, the Mosaic law represents the old covenant; Jesus Christ came, he said, to institute "the new covenant in my blood, which is poured out for you" (Luke 22 v 20; 1 Corinthians 11 v 23-25). We are people of the new covenant, in Christ.[11]

Even though it's been fulfilled, the old covenant still reflects the character of God who gave it. The God of

---

11 For a general introduction to law in Scripture, see T.D. Alexander's "Law," in the *New International Version Zondervan Study Bible*, edited D.A. Carson (Zondervan, 2015), pages 2649-2651.

the Bible is one God, whose purpose has always been to redeem a people for himself through his Son. He's a God who saves—never through human obedience to the law but always and only through faith in him, by his mercy and grace. But here is our question: how do we see the character of this gracious, merciful God reflected in some of the harder details of his law?

Parts of this law are really hard to understand. Some of the "cases" to which it speaks are strange and full of ugliness—they're a lot like stepping into dark places filled with fearful shadows. Deuteronomy 21 v 10-14 is a vivid example:

> *When you go to war against your enemies and the LORD your God delivers them into your hands and you take captives, if you notice among the captives a beautiful woman and are attracted to her, you may take her as your wife. Bring her into your home and have her shave her head, trim her nails and put aside the clothes she was wearing when captured. After she has lived in your house and mourned her father and mother for a full month, then you may go to her and be her husband and she shall be your wife. If you are not pleased with her, let her go wherever she wishes. You must not sell her or treat her as a slave, since you have dishonored her.*[12]

Just the first sentence makes us recoil, as we're plunged into this dark period when Israel warred with surrounding

---

[12] The first time these verses struck me was in a church class taught by Daniel Block, who wrote *Deuteronomy* in the NIV Application Commentary series (Zondervan, 2012); see especially pages 494-496, which have helped me in this discussion. Dr. Block unpacks the laws about women with compassion and, even more, with appreciation for God's compassion and mercy evident in this case law given to protect those in the most vulnerable circumstances. I've also learned from a workshop given by Mary Willson at The Gospel Coalition Women's Conference in 2016: http://resources.thegospelcoalition.org/library/is-god-a-misogynist (accessed 10/3/17).

nations. The scenario reeks with sin: the "case" of this "case law" is the horrific circumstance of a woman being torn from family and home, and forced as a prisoner of war to marry her captor.

So, why does this horrific case appear in God's law? It's important to say clearly, first, that God is not endorsing the taking of women captive; the context here is descriptive, not prescriptive. The capturing of women in war or in any context is sin, dreadful sin. Case laws speak into a desperately fallen world, restraining sin and protecting people in the midst of it.

We can understand this better by listening to Jesus' explanation, in a conversation with the Pharisees about another Old Testament case law: one dealing with another painful situation—divorce. Deuteronomy 24 addresses a case in which a man writes a "certificate of divorce" and sends his wife away (Deuteronomy 24 v 1-4). The Pharisees knew this part of the law and asked Jesus a trick question about it: "Is it lawful for a man to divorce his wife for any and every reason?" (Matthew 19 v 3). We've seen Jesus' first response in chapters 1 and 2 of this book—he quoted Genesis 1 v 27 and 2 v 24, affirming God's original, unchanging good plan for the marriage of a man and a woman that God joins together and that no one must separate.

But (sort of like us, perhaps!) the Pharisees weren't satisfied:

> *"Why then," they asked, "did Moses command that a man give his wife a certificate of divorce and send her away?"*
>
> *Jesus replied, "Moses permitted you to divorce your wives because your hearts were hard. But it was not this way from the beginning." (Matthew 19 v 7-8)*

Jesus explains that the law in cases of divorce addressed a fallen world, full of hard hearts. Such laws did not condone sin, but rather presupposed the existence of sin; and they showed God's merciful character in the midst of it. God not only commanded his people to live holy and sinless lives, but he also made a way to deal with the times when they fell short of his demands. God's ultimate mercy is revealed in his Son, who came to deal finally with our falling short: Jesus perfectly fulfilled the law in his life, and then offered himself as the perfect sacrifice for our sin in his death.

A Case of God's Mercy

As we press into Deuteronomy 21 v 10-14, then, the helpful question to ask is this: in the midst of the hard hearts of warring peoples, how did God show his merciful character? First of all, according to this case law, the way in which the Israelites took women captives was to differ dramatically from the way surrounding nations treated the women of conquered peoples. In Near-Eastern cultures rape was common; in war, rape was expected. Women were routinely and brutally abused on the battlefield and in the homes to which they were taken. When the effects of sin that were declared back in Genesis 3 play out through history, the dominating rule of men is manifest in colors of bruises and cries of pain. We must acknowledge that, in our world today, both private and overt domination persists, through sex trafficking, or domestic abuse, or wars on whole human populations, and on and on.

But God's case law limits the outworkings of sin in this situation. For an Israelite man who saw and desired a woman among the captives, sexual relations outside of marriage were not an option. Sex within marriage was the only option: "You may take her as your wife" (Deuteronomy 21 v 11). The law upheld the dignity of human beings created in the image of God, male and female, and made by God to become one flesh as husband and wife.

But, you may well be asking, why didn't God forbid not just the rape but the capture of women, period? Why did he allow for such hard hearts among his people, for so long? Why did he wait all those centuries before sending his Son? I don't know. But there's one thing we can know: God's purposes are redemptive. From the beginning, as we've seen, God had a plan to redeem this fallen world and all the people in it who turn to him in faith. He worked that plan through the nation of Israel. Let's keep peering into these laws, and we'll glimpse our rescuing God more clearly.

Not only were rape and brutality not options, but certain practices leading up to the marriage were required—practices that valued and protected a captured woman in every way possible. The head-shaving, nail-trimming, and changing of clothes seem demeaning, and yet this process, according to Paul Copan, allowed her "a transition period to make an outer and inner break from her past way of life. Only after this could she be taken as a wife."[13] She must be given at least a full month, says the law, to mourn her father and mother (v 13). Whether or not her own family members have died in the war, she has lost them and must grieve that loss. These safeguards acknowledge and respect the grief of this woman's situation; the law calls all those involved to see her as a human being who has not been well-treated up to now, and who from this point onwards must be compassionately treated.

Further, should the man change his mind, the law stipulates that the woman should not be treated as a slave;

---

13 *Is God a Moral Monster?*, page 120.

she cannot be sold but instead must be allowed freedom to go where she wishes. She cannot be "dishonored" or taken against her will again. The law exists to put a guard of protection around her, even when the hard-hearted world around her has rejected the guards put in place from the beginning. God's merciful hand is not absent, even when he allows sinful hands to do their work for a time. In this case, says God, the man who takes her home must take responsibility to care for her in a way that acknowledges her personhood.

There's more mercy here. The law exists also to allow for God's people to include a foreign woman by making her part of God's family, just as happened in the more famous cases of Rahab and Ruth. Both of those women were from nations which were enemies of God's people: Rahab from Jericho (Joshua 2 v 1-3) and Ruth from Moab (Ruth 1 v 1-5). Their stories were very different from those of these captive women: both Rahab and Ruth came to faith in the God of Israel and then chose to join his people. They experienced the harsh reality of sin among their own people and a dramatic parting with their homelands, but they embraced that parting in order to follow the one true God. In contrast, a captive was torn away from her people before knowing God. But it remains the case that she was invited to know him and become part of his people.

So for a captive woman, the weeks of saying good-bye to her past were intended to be also a time of learning about her present and coming to embrace the reality of joining this new nation. This process would make her a legitimate part of God's covenant community, a full member of the people whom God had promised to bless, and through whom God would bless the world. She would have access to knowing God through his revealed word and to worshiping him in the way that word prescribed. In other words, God put this woman in the place of blessing. Agonizing blessing it was, wrought through sin we would never condone and suffering we can't imagine—but blessing it was.

Looking back from the perspective of heaven, God's people from all times and places will have different stories to tell of how God brought them into his family— and those stories will always involve sin—our own first, and also that of others. Those women captives who by faith received God's gift of eternal life will be able to testify to an inexplicable providence, so deeply full of suffering, but eternally full of grace. The Lord Jesus knows all this suffering—Jesus the Son of God, who took on our sin and suffered the depths of God's wrath in our place, to give us life.

Laws and Grace

God's grace is present in the Old Testament laws concerning women, both in the big picture and even in the smallest and most personal details. Signs of grace are to be found, for example, in the ceremonial laws concerning menstrual periods and childbirth. Why would God call a woman "unclean" when she has her monthly period? Why would God give a law stating that, "when a woman has her regular flow of blood, the impurity of her monthly period will last seven days, and anyone who touches her will be unclean till evening" (Leviticus 15 v 19)? Two things help us here: first, if we read all of Leviticus 15, we find equal attention given to men's reproductive discharges, with equal contamination and equal requirements for purification. God's not out to get women; he's seeking to communicate something about cleanness and uncleanness among all people. And that something doesn't just have to do with protection of his people from diseases easily communicated through blood and semen, though that was one good effect of these laws.

The second, larger, point is this: through these ceremonial laws God was communicating his holiness and his mercy. We have to read through Leviticus to grasp the detailed requirements for purification and blood sacrifice, all of which point to the way our sin disqualifies us from approaching a holy God. For us to come before such a God in worship, sin must be dealt with—and God mercifully provided a way.

Discharges of blood and semen in themselves are not evil. These discharges were symbols of uncleanness. Blood in itself represents life: "The life of every creature is its blood" (Leviticus 17 v 14). So the loss of blood, as in a woman's bleeding, was directly associated with death— death that came on the human race as God's judgment for sin. These Old Testament purification rituals point backward to the fall and point forward to the Lord Jesus, who shed his blood to cleanse us from our sin and give us eternal life. In chapter 8, we'll see Jesus welcoming a desperate woman with a chronic discharge of blood who had, in faith, touched him and been healed by him. These Old Testament laws help us grasp the beauty of that scene.

All this leads to one reasonable explanation for a requirement in Leviticus 12 v 1-8 that might appear to be a straightforwardly sexist case: a woman had to remain apart and "impure" twice as long after the birth of a daughter (eighty days) as after the birth of a son (forty days). Clearly the mother's post-partum bleeding would be the same in either case. Why the different durations? Well, possibly because the daughter, a female, would also be associated with blood through her monthly periods. It's also possible that the lengthier exclusion of female children from the temple emphasized the Israelites' separation from the fertility rites and cult prostitution common in Canaanite temples.[14]

We'll talk more about childbearing in chapter 6, but for now, we can begin to see how the details of these Old Testament laws concerning women, as we peer into them, show glimmers of grace-filled light.

A Dark Period: Judges and Jephthah

All these laws didn't make God's people holy. One of the bleakest periods of Old Testament history comes after the entrance of God's people into the promised land, during the time when judges ruled—and God's laws were forgotten. The book of Judges' repeated, echoing description captures the situation: "In those days there was no king in Israel. Everyone did what was right in his own eyes" (17 v 6; 21 v 25, ESV). *Description* is the key word for these distressing narratives: the evil actions of God's people are not prescribed or commended as examples to follow, but rather described as proof of the downward-spiraling patterns of sinful rebellion against God. Each leader and each episode in this book is worse than the last. What was right in the people's own eyes just brought more and more "evil in the eyes of the LORD" (2 v 11; 3 v 7; 3 v 12; 4 v 1; 6 v 1; 10 v 6; 13 v 1).

Judges shows with vivid drama the grievous effects of the fall. Just as God had declared back in Genesis 3, these effects are tragically played out in how women and men treat each other. In the story of Samson, for example, we see a strong man brought down by a woman whose desire

---

14 *Is God a Moral Monster?*, page 106. Copan also offers another suggestion: a daughter is further associated with blood through a slight vaginal discharge of blood common in newborn girls, "due to the withdrawal of the mother's estrogen when the infant girl exits the mother's womb."

is against him. In the story of Jephthah, we see a helpless young woman "ruled" mercilessly by her father.

Jephthah's is a story almost too hard to take. The basic plot in Judges 11 is clear—and shocking. Jephthah, whom God used as a mighty warrior against Israel's enemies, makes an inexplicably rash vow: if God will let him destroy the enemy Ammonites in battle, he will sacrifice as a burnt offering whatever (or whoever; the referent is disputed) comes first out of his door when he returns victorious (11 v 30-31). Was he expecting an animal that he might sacrifice, or was he following the example of the very nations he led Israel to conquer, in the practice of human sacrifice to appease angry gods?[15] The Bible does not say. What it does say is that when Jephthah's daughter comes out to meet him, dancing to the sound of timbrels, he does not turn back from his rash vow (as God's law actually provided for; see Leviticus 5 v 4-6). You would think that Jephthah, himself a rejected illegitimate son, would have done anything in the world to protect his only child, a daughter. Instead, after granting her two months in which to weep with her friends over her childless end, "he did to her as he had vowed" (11 v 39).

This is dark, very dark. And it only gets worse.

In the Days Without a King

The final and bleakest section of this most bleak of biblical books begins in chapter 19 with a journeying Levite, a member of the Israelite tribe designated by God to serve as religious leaders for his people. This Levite and his concubine (a kind of long-term mistress) stay overnight

---

15 Human sacrifice (and child sacrifice in particular) was explicitly forbidden in the law God had given to his people: see Leviticus 18 v 21; 20 v 1-5; Deuteronomy 12 v 31; 18 v 10.

in Gibeah, where he expects to find safety with inhabitants who are fellow Israelites, from the tribe of Benjamin. But there is no safety. When threatened at his host's door by a gang of Benjamites who are clamoring to rape him, this Levite sends his concubine out to be raped and abused all night long. He finds her in the morning clinging to the threshold, and simply says to her, "Get up; let's go." Having loaded her on his donkey and traveled home, he then cuts up her dead body "limb by limb, into twelve parts," which he sends throughout Israel (19 v 22-29).

Even as I type those words, it's hard all over again to believe that they are in the Bible, describing the actions of people called by God to be his. This is shocking and repulsive. How could God allow it?

The worst is saved for last, here in Judges, and the worst involves this horrific treatment of a woman—by one who was supposed to be a religious leader. The story of a raging gang at the door, intent upon rape, brings echoes of the evil city of Sodom (Genesis 19 v 1-9)—only this is not Sodom; these are Israelites. And that's the point: God's own people have come this low. Without a king, and bent upon doing what is right in their own eyes, fallen human beings will increasingly destroy one another, and men will destroy women in the cruelest ways. The original creation of human beings in the image of God showed them in perfect harmony as male and female. Their deepest rebellion brings the ugliest turning inside out of that harmony.

There's no real resolution in Judges—only further evil, even further rape. The book concludes, "In those days there was no king in Israel. Everyone did what was right in his own eyes" (Judges 21 v 25, ESV).

This book (and the whole Bible) asks us to open our eyes and see the world not as we imagine it to be, but as it is: fallen, full of sin, desperately in need of rescue. The wonder is that this book (and the whole Bible) points us toward that rescue. Hard as it is to imagine, the people in Judges really are the people through whom God promised to work his grand rescue of the human race. We glimpse God's rescuing nature as we read. Throughout Judges, when God's people rebel, his anger burns against their sin, and he gives them into the hand of enemy nations. What is truly remarkable, though, is that each time God's people turn back to him and cry out, he hears them. He cares about their misery. He raises up deliverers from among them. He has mercy. His mercy reaches this far down.

Judges is a book about God's rescue of his sinful people again and again, through horribly imperfect saviors who leave us longing for the perfect One. That Savior delivers his people forever, from all their enemies; he saves them from their sin by himself bearing the wrath of God that they deserve. The Old Testament vividly shows the need for such a Savior, such a King.

Seeing the Light in the Dark

The Old Testament is full of dark places. In those places we find many women suffering, often at the hands of men. And we grieve to see them. The more we look, the more we make out a stretching shadowy landscape crowded with human beings, male and female, all living out the brokenness of the fall. We see ourselves in that crowd.

Yet as we peer into the dark, we find God's mercy glimmering. We remember the promise of the seed, back in Eden. We know and marvel that God accomplished this promise through the nation of Israel. And we celebrate the fact that in Christ the promise has been fulfilled—the light has come into this world. Through God's own Son the rescue has been accomplished.

The world still has deep dark places. So do our own lives. Sin and death have been conquered but not yet banished. Even so we can walk on in the light, by faith—for God is not dark; he is light. Our merciful God has rescued us from the dark.

Strong Women

I grew up not really thinking about what a strong woman my mother is. She was just my mom—straightforward, down to earth, demanding, always ready to encourage my dad and my sister and me, and ever busy with various kinds of work.

Mom taught 6th grade at the school I attended. It didn't seem unusual to glimpse her in the faculty lounge or standing in front of a classroom or grading papers at her desk. She directed the church choir for years. It didn't seem strange to me to see her up there every Sunday waving her arms and leading a group of around forty men and women. She was also a great cook. She and my dad developed optimal efficiency in working together to host meal after meal, especially for students or guests at the seminary where my father taught. Dad was an unbelievably fast potato-peeler, dishwasher-loader, and all-round supporter of my mother's gifts. She was given a lot of them. Looking back, I see even more clearly that she used them well. She was, and is, a strong godly woman.

Yes to Strong Women

My goal in this chapter is to cry out a resounding "Yes!" to strong godly women as a gift from God. If you're reading this and you consider yourself a strong woman, perhaps with leadership gifts, there's a chance you're struggling to find your place in the church. Please don't conclude there's not a place for you.

Genesis 1 and 2 showed us an ordered relationship between man and woman, and we shall see more of that order in chapters 9 and 10 as the New Testament speaks specifically to marriage and to the church. As we proceed we must be careful to avoid two extremes: on the one hand, the extreme of taking God's order too lightly, and on the other hand, the extreme of using God's order to impose rules and regulations that go beyond what the Bible actually says. For example, we take God's order too lightly if we speak of our identity only in terms of being made in God's image, minimizing the importance of being distinctly male or female image-bearers.

But we can easily move toward the opposite extreme: we can so fixate on male/female distinctions that they harden into categories that separate instead of complementing, and that confine instead of fostering growth in God's image. A number of women stand out in Scripture and help us learn to avoid these extremes. Deborah from the book of Judges is one of them, and she is our main focus in this chapter. Deborah doesn't fit some of the categories sometimes associated with women who are submissive to God's word and God's order. But we'll see that she actually embraces God's word and God's order. In fact, the big idea of Judges 4 and 5 is not the greatness of a woman but the greatness of the Lord God she serves. Deborah offers a hugely encouraging example of a strong woman who serves the Lord, who respects and exhorts the male leaders around her, and who wholeheartedly embraces the work God puts before her.

Deborah challenges us to consider that the existence

of an ordered creation of male and female equally in the image of God leaves more room for the growth and strength of men and women alike than most of us are in the habit of imagining. Sometimes Deborah is ignored, or even worried about a little, by those who want to affirm ordered roles of male and female in marriage and in the church. On the other hand, sometimes Deborah is paraded a bit by those who want to affirm equality in roles as well as in the essential image-bearing value of men and women. Neither of those approaches works.

Let's take a close-up look at Deborah as the writer of Judges presents her. She is the fourth named judge in the book, introduced without much commentary: "Now Deborah, a prophetess, the wife of Lappidoth, was judging Israel at that time" (Judges 4 v 4, ESV). We'll talk about her prophetic role in a moment, but it is her judging role that is emphasized at the start. She "held court under the Palm of Deborah ... and the Israelites went up to her to have their disputes decided." It was unusual for a woman to be judging in Israel; all the judges surrounding Deborah in this book are men. She definitely stands out. The beauty of Deborah is that she stands out not as a poor fill-in but as arguably the most godly leader in the book of Judges.

Deborah is also introduced as a wife, but we're not told anything about her husband Lappidoth, whether they had children, or how God wove together their various life stages and responsibilities. In Deborah's song (Judges 5) she identifies herself as "a mother in Israel" (5 v 7)— probably a metaphorical description: one that beautifully pictures Deborah's role of raising up and sustaining those around her in the family of God's people. Scripture shines its light on the way Deborah actively served that larger family, as she gave herself to serving the Lord God.

Real Strength: Serving God in Hard Times

Deborah was an active servant of God in a truly challenging context. Her world was full of the worst kinds of moral and cultural debasement. We saw something of the miserable context of Judges in the last chapter; we know the kind of evil that was growing among God's own people. Deborah was serving God while surrounded by many who were not. Judges 4 begins with the refrain, "Again the Israelites did evil in the eyes of the Lord" (4 v 1)—and this time the Lord had given them into the hand of the Canaanite king and his military commander Sisera. God's people were suffering under the cruel oppression of Sisera with his 900 iron chariots. This was a man who held the surrounding nations' prevailing view of women as the "spoil" of battle—"a womb or two for every man" (5 v 30, ESV). In the middle of all this turbulence, there sits Deborah under her tree, steadily administering God's justice. It's an amazing picture.

In raising up Deborah and in including this story in his inspired word, God is sending a greatly encouraging message concerning women and their potential to serve God actively even in the midst of the worst evil. We've seen that when evil is unrestrained, women often become the victims of oppression by cruel men. And yet some of the brightest light in the darkest parts of salvation history shines from women who were called to serve God and who did so faithfully, playing a crucial part in the story of redemption.

We might think of Rahab, similarly surrounded—in her case by a whole city of unbelievers in Jericho who practiced the worst kinds of evils on one another (see Joshua 2). Rahab herself was a prostitute, participating in the sinful culture of which she was a part. How amazing that of all the people in Jericho God should draw this woman to himself. By his grace, Rahab turned her allegiance to the one true God, acted out that allegiance by protecting the spies sent from God's people, and finally joined that people, becoming part of the line of those from whom would come the promised Savior.

A few generations later, in the time of the judges, Ruth emerged from a godless culture and heard the call to follow the one true God. In God's providence she met and married into a family of God's people sojourning in her country of Moab—and later as a widow accompanied her also-widowed mother-in-law back to Bethlehem in Judah. The book named after her gives a vivid glimpse of God's good hand on his people even through this dark period of disobedience, and specifically through strong, godly servants like Ruth and Boaz, the man who loved and protected this godly woman. These are all lights in the dark. The very existence of a Ruth or Rahab or Deborah in the midst of such challenging contexts certainly shows a lot about these women of faith—and it shows even more about the faithful God they trusted and served.

What kind of context has God given you in which to serve him? You may be blessed by godly, encouraging people all around you—or you may well be facing ungodly attitudes and actions that fill your path with struggle day by day. Maybe it's co-workers who scorn your values, or maybe it's the invasion of pornography into your home and family. Close to home and in the culture surrounding us, as believers we live constantly confronted by all sorts of "evil in the eyes of the LORD." The stories of women like Deborah can remind us of the ways in which God uses faithful individuals, including strong godly women, for his good purposes in the midst of the darkest circumstances.

But what was the source of Deborah's strength? None of us is good or strong on our own. Deborah did not pretend to be. Strong as she was, Deborah wasn't out to emerge from the shadows as some super-strong, shining heroine. We can be glad of that, we normal, sinful human beings. We need to hear this woman's story and see just how she brought light into the dark part of history in which God placed her.

Serving God by Speaking His Word

Deborah was an active servant of God in the midst of a dark world *by faithfully declaring his word.* She is called "a prophet" (NIV) or "prophetess" (ESV)—one who brought God's word to the people God indicated. Deborah was not unique in this—other women exercised prophetic gifts in Old Testament times. Miriam, Moses' sister, was another leader and prophetess—and one who also sang a song (Exodus 15 v 20-21). King Josiah of Judah sent Hilkiah the priest to inquire of Huldah the prophetess (2 Kings 22 v 14). The prophet Isaiah's wife is called a prophetess (Isaiah 8 v 3). As we'll discuss in chapter 10, Scripture's whole trajectory affirms women and men together in the activity of prophesying (see Acts 2 v 14-21 with Joel 2 v 28-32; 1 Corinthians 11 v 4-5).

Now, to be a spokesperson for God does not automatically infer godliness; God did speak through a donkey (Numbers 22 v 28). In Deborah's case, we can see her speaking God's words with evident faithfulness and strength. It's no accident that the Holy Spirit inspired her to write (perhaps with Barak, perhaps alone) a song of praise to the Lord that takes a prominent place in this story and forever in the Scriptures, in Judges 5. Deborah loves the Lord and calls others to that same love; she ends her song with these uplifting words addressed to the Lord God:

> *May all who love you be like the sun*
>> *when it rises in its strength. (Judges 5 v 31)*

Throughout the story, Deborah evidences constant awareness of God. Her words are full of him and his words. To my shame, and perhaps because I had been concentrating so much just on Deborah in my thinking, I had forgotten how relentlessly about God this story is! Deborah sends for Barak in order to give him not her command, but God's command: "The LORD, the God of Israel, commands you…" (4 v 6). She is not the commander; she is the one who communicates God's message—that's what prophets did. At the crucial point of military attack, Deborah's cry to action is about what God is doing: "Go! This is the day the LORD has given Sisera into your hands. Has not the LORD gone ahead of you?" (4 v 14). And when Barak leads the charge, we are told exactly who achieved the victory: "At Barak's advance, the LORD routed Sisera and all his chariots and army by the sword" (v 15). This is a story about an amazing God. He's a God who pours out his word and then accomplishes it unfailingly.

And God chose in this case to pour out his revelation through Deborah, who communicates it powerfully and beautifully. We find out in Deborah's song that God brought storms and rain, which made all Sisera's heavy chariots get stuck in the mud. Her song not only unfolds the events of nature; it reveals the awesome God of nature—it's on him that Deborah's eyes are fixed, and she shows him to us through her words. Deborah says she will "sing to the LORD" (5 v 3), and then she does it, vividly and personally. She pictures God marching out to war, shaking the earth and making the mountains quake and the heavens pour out water. The imagery (along with a reference to Sinai) echoes language often used in Scripture to describe God's deliverance of his people from Egypt by parting the Red Sea. Deborah has taken in deeply the history of God's saving works; that history echoes in this powerful poetry, exalting the Lord who comes to deliver his people:

> *When you, LORD, went out from Seir,*
>   *when you marched from the land of Edom,*
> *the earth shook, the heavens poured,*
>   *the clouds poured down water.*
> *The mountains quaked before the LORD, the One of Sinai,*
>   *before the LORD, the God of Israel. (5 v 4-5)*

If there is anything we want to learn from Deborah, it's to have our minds and words filled with the Lord God. Deborah was given the great gift of being a prophet and speaking God's word directly; today, we have been given God's completed word in the Scriptures, so that every one of us can feed on it and love it and let it flavor and shape all the words we give to others, in every context where God calls us to speak.

What a mercy that when the fall occurred, God didn't stop speaking to us human beings. He didn't leave us in dead silence. He kept giving his words and his promises—all of which shine forth the truth of deliverance that happened finally through his Son, the Word made flesh (John 1 v 1, 14). The Bible is not a collection of dry, academic truths to be learned; it is God speaking to us, revealing himself to us, in living and active words breathed out by his Spirit. Deborah points us to set our hearts on the living God who reveals himself through living words. How much do you live on these words? Are you feeding on them so deeply and regularly that you have stores to feed the hungry ones around you? When you speak his words, does your love for our awesome Lord God come through?

Serving God by Serving Leaders

Deborah actively served God in a truly challenging context by faithfully declaring his word *and by serving well the leaders around her.* There is utter clarity in Deborah's call from the Lord to Barak to deliver God's people from their enemies in battle. She respects and embraces Barak's role as deliverer of his people. Barak is the one who is listed along with several other judges in Hebrews 11 v 32—and I don't think Deborah would have minded that. In fact, that's what Deborah was after: she called Barak to take the leadership God had declared for him. This is a woman who not only delivers God's word but acts on it. When Barak refuses to go to battle without her (4 v 8), she agrees with no hesitation to accompany him; she is willing to be a helper to him. She is a raiser-up of Israel's leaders.

Deborah does give God's word of judgment on Barak's somewhat hesitant response; Barak is asking for more assurance than simply God's word, and because of that, Deborah tells him, "The LORD will deliver Sisera into the hands of a woman" (4 v 9). Whatever we think about such a judgment from our vantage point now, from the vantage point of that time and place this judgment would have brought shame on Barak. Military leadership belonged to men, and this military job should have belonged to him as leader.

There is an undeniable male/female tension throughout this story, and the point of the tension is not to undermine the women (who are presented as brave and faithful) but rather to call out the men (who weren't stepping up to their leadership roles). Deborah's song makes it even more clear. She begins positively, praising God for those times when male leaders do lead:

When the princes in Israel take the lead,
*   when the people willingly offer themselves—*
*   praise the LORD! (Judges 5 v 2)*

Her song is full of praise for the men from tribes who showed up for battle, but she is not afraid to call out the tribes who *didn't* show up, not only reproaching them but giving God's severe judgment on them for not coming out "to help the LORD against the mighty" (5 v 23).

By contrast, then, the song exalts Jael, the woman who fulfilled God's prophetic judgment upon Barak back in 4 v 9 as she hammered a tent peg through Sisera's temple. I know that sounds pretty violent and gory to us. But I know, too, that most of us find a sort of pleasure in Jael's facility with hammers and tent pegs, these tools of the women's work of setting up the tents. In Deborah's eyes, Jael's action was part of the deliverance of God's people from their enemies, and Jael, "most blessed of women," gets the honor of a play-by-play retelling of the scene in Deborah's song:

Most blessed of women be Jael,
*   the wife of Heber the Kenite,*
*   most blessed of tent-dwelling women.*
He asked for water, and she gave him milk;
*   in a bowl fit for nobles she brought him curdled milk.*
Her hand reached for the tent peg,
*   her right hand to the workman's hammer.*
She struck Sisera, she crushed his head,
*   she shattered and pierced his temple.*
At her feet he sank,
*   he fell; there he lay.*
At her feet he sank, he fell;
*   where he sank, there he fell—dead. (5 v 24-27)*

Nobody who reads Judges is going to forget this scene! Jael wields the hammer, and Deborah wields the words; the battering of quick repetitive phrases lets us feel the mallet's blows. These two women frame the story of chapter 4 and the song of chapter 5; it's a frame of strong women who serve the Lord, surrounding a bunch of not-strong men who are not all in.

Deborah was a "mother in Israel"; with her life-filled words she was aiming to raise up its princes. "My heart is with Israel's princes," she sang (5 v 9). She served as a helper to God's designated leaders in the strongest way possible, according to the gifts God gave her, in the context in which he placed her. Deborah perhaps could have given up on Barak and led the troops out herself; I think there's a good chance she would have done it brilliantly. But she didn't take over the job to which God had called Barak; instead, she raised him up, called him to God's word, cared about him, exhorted him, and praised God when Barak and other leaders in Israel responded (v 2).

Usually in a discussion of church-based ministry among women, in the process of talking about ways to nurture and benefit from strong, word-filled women, the subject of the men comes up. In my experience, the comments follow a predictable path. Men in the congregation aren't stepping up to leadership. Many of them are not growing in the word as quickly as many of the women. It's hard to find qualified leaders. Such comments point to the fact that most churches definitely need more attention to ministry among men, along with growing and thriving ministry among women.

The factors contributing to this need are surely complex. In contexts where elders and pastors are male, some congregations tend to focus biblical training just on that group of men in leadership, instead of training up all the members of the church. Perhaps sometimes even among elders there is not careful training in the word that can be passed on to others. Among men who are not elders, some may be preoccupied with work matters and therefore leave spiritual matters to others who seem to have more time. Some husbands may be intimidated by wives who are growing in Christ and in his word. The answer, of course, is not to stifle women's growth but rather to encourage and enable growth among all the men—indeed, among the whole congregation.

Women can help here in crucial ways. Deborah models a strong, godly encouragement of the leaders God has called. It's a good thing at times for us women to ask for more leadership, or more substantive leadership, from pastors and elders—or to discuss with them areas of concern. We should be praying for and actively building up both potential and actual male leaders in our midst—having a heart for the "princes of Israel," so to speak. There are extremes to avoid: being manipulative or intrusive, on the one hand, and shrinking into some kind of stereotypically passive role, on the other. Either extreme is unattractive, unhelpful, and unbiblical. Deborah's humble, God-centered example guards against both. If it's true, as we'll later discuss, that qualified men are the God-ordained spiritual leaders of the church, then those leaders need women to be actively for them, for the sake of God's people.

If you are reading this as a man in leadership—in marriage and/or in the church—I pray the story of Deborah will encourage you. How might you be helping those around you, including women and men, to grow in the word and in the Lord? How might you be listening better to those around you, including women and men, who can share the Lord's wisdom with you? How might you be encouraging and enabling both women and men to serve effectively among God's people? As you take godly leadership, by God's grace, may the men and women and children of God's family grow and thrive, for the glory of Christ our Lord.

Serving by Singing

Finally, let's not miss the fact that, in the midst of it all, Deborah serves by singing! She writes and sings of the beauty of the story God is authoring, with all its tension and struggle; ultimately, she sings of her wonder at the ways of God. She sees the marvel of the weaving of this God-ordained plot, with Sisera wandering into the tent of a woman named Jael—and she sings it to the glory of the Lord. Actually, she and Barak together sing this song to the people. It is a part of Deborah's ministry to them.

Not only that, but Deborah is willing to challenge those who would pass by and pay no attention to such songs:

> *You who ride on white donkeys,*
> *sitting on your saddle blankets,*
> *and you who walk along the road,*
> *consider the voice of the singers at the watering places.*
> *They recite the victories of the* Lord,
> *the victories of his villagers in Israel. (5 v 10-11)*

It's easy to be tempted to "ride by" Deborah's story without stopping to digest in detail both the story and the song. Perhaps we'd be less argumentative and more convicted in heart if we took the time to hear the heart of Deborah in her song. We should "consider the voice of the singers."

Why does God give us so many songs and so much poetry in the Scriptures? These musical words have a way of powerfully piercing our imaginations and our hearts. Psalms and hymns and spiritual songs help us step back and see with larger vision the stories we're living in: all part of the story directed by God. They help us seek God. And they help us praise him for his good and sovereign direction. In her carefully chosen words, Deborah turned the people's eyes to the wonders of God's works. We might be led to wonder where our words point people's eyes—whether in songs or prayers or notes or even just conversational comments.

What will you take away from Deborah? Along with wonder at the work of God, let it be a resounding "Yes!" to God's gift of strong godly women, then and now. Deborah had qualities that we can pray the women and daughters of our church will have, for it is God himself who, by his grace and through his Spirit, grows these qualities. If you're that strong woman I mentioned at the start of this chapter—perhaps with leadership gifts, perhaps struggling to find your place in the church—let it be an encouragement that God has made you and given you your gifts so that you might joyfully serve him among his people.

We can pray, and we can with God's help do everything possible both to become and to nurture other modern-day Deborahs who are strong in the Lord, speaking his word without fear and with humility. We can pray and encourage believing women to serve actively according to God's word, in every role and pathway he opens to them. We can pray for and help cultivate hearts full of respect, prayer, and encouragement for God's ordained spiritual leaders of the church.

And we can pray that God's word would so fill the minds and hearts of modern-day Deborahs that it will come out in songs of praise! May God's word permeate all of our thoughts and words and songs, for the glory of Christ and the blessing of his people.

Women, Sex, and a Question of Double Standards

" S o much for 'thou shalt not commit adultery.'"

The *New York Daily News* offered this verdict in 2014, reporting on survey results from "Ashley Madison," a web-based service that helps married people find partners for extra-marital affairs. The survey revealed that a quarter of their users self-identified as "evangelical"—by far the highest percentage among all responders.[16] The truth was painfully evident when in 2015 Ashley Madison's online accounts were hacked and names of over 30 million users of their services were publicly shared.

People were shocked and embarrassed by all this, but not *that* shocked or even *that* embarrassed. We've seen too much. How many dozens of movie and TV scenes have drawn in even Christians, numbing our minds to the fact that we were watching extramarital sex? (Not only watching, but feeling happy for heroes and heroines in love who consummate something that isn't a marriage.) What of

---

16 Victoria Taylor, "Evangelicals are the least faithful when it comes to spouses, survey suggests," nydailynews.com, June 3, 2014, http://nydn.us/1li3IAn, accessed 10/3/17.

our friend, the successful Christian business owner who left his wife for another woman—but who maintains his success, gives generously to the community, and provides good jobs for many people... don't we tend, after a while, to minimize or forget about his adultery? What of the many students who simply can't understand why Christians would hold on to antiquated sexual standards that clearly represent only repression—and that seem unnecessary with the advent of birth control?

American-based websites that quantify such behavior generally report that in around one third of all marriages one or both of the partners say they've cheated on the other.[17] One UK news source reports that barely a third of British men and women think an extra-marital affair puts strain on the relationship; in other words, it's not that big of a problem.[18] But if you are reading this and you have experienced adultery in one way or another, you know statistics don't tell it all. You may be experiencing the grief of being betrayed, or perhaps the guilt of betraying. You may be in a relationship, not married, and struggling to figure out how sex and commitment go together—or don't go together.

We've seen in Genesis the God who designed us as male and female from the beginning; we know he cares about these issues in detail. We know he set up marriage between a man and a woman and blessed that union. We know the seventh of the Ten Commandments, plain and unadulterated: "You shall not commit adultery" (Exodus 20 v 14). And yet we Christians struggle with issues of sexual ethics; we struggle with living out sexual purity, and we struggle

---

17 "Infidelity Statistics 2017: Why, When, and How People Stray," February 1, 2017, trustify.info/blog/infidelity-statistics-2017, accessed 5/25/17.

18 John Bingham, "Adultery Not a Problem for Most Britons," *The Daily Telegraph*, 2/12/15, http://bit.ly/2fHqPam, accessed 10/3/17.

with talking about it. We might waver: in the Ashley Madison era, are we just way too judgmental? Should we really continue to hold the view that sexual relations are a gift from God intended only for a man and a woman within the bonds of marriage? We might wonder: should these issues perhaps just be resolved privately and individually before God, who surely understands our needs and desires our happiness?

It's with all this in mind that I want to invite you to join the crowd surrounding Jesus as a woman is dragged alone before him—a woman deserving death by stoning, say her accusers, according to the Law of Moses. Their question to Jesus hangs in the air: "Now what do you say?" (John 8 v 5). And there she stands, this woman, head down, waiting for his response.

What Kind of Mercy?

Although this passage does not appear in the earliest manuscripts, most of our Bibles include John 7 v 53 – 8 v 11, as most scholars take these verses as a true encounter, if not a legitimate part of the Scriptures. The scene takes place in the temple courts, with all the people gathered around to hear Jesus teach. It's a vivid, emotion-filled scene—probably a shocking one for many today who might find it hard even to imagine a woman being stoned for adultery. But in come the teachers of the law and the Pharisees (all the Old Testament experts) with this woman, whom they set before the whole group and accuse of being caught in the act of adultery. Most of us might have for many years taken without question the Pharisees' words:

In the Law Moses commanded us to stone such women.

(8 v 5)

Here we are again at the Old Testament law.[19] And we must ask: are the Pharisees representing well God's instructions given through Moses? The scene feels brutally harsh, and what these Pharisees say sounds unfair and sexist. Here is this woman dragged alone in shame before this group in the temple courts and accused of a sin that clearly involved two people. When she was caught in the act (v 4), there must have been a man with whom she was acting! Did he run off? Did they let him go? Are they telling the truth? Why do these men say only that the law condemns such *women*?

Jesus doesn't condemn this woman. He bends down and starts to write on the ground with his finger. He's quiet, but the proud law-enforcers keep demanding a response. They don't really care about this woman or about keeping the law; they're just "using this question as a trap, in order to have a basis for accusing him" (v 6). How ironic: we said in chapter 4 that the Old Testament law reflects the character of the God who gave it. Here in this scene is the same God, in the flesh, and these men aim to use his law to undermine, accuse, and destroy him. But their trap remains unsprung. Jesus finally straightens up and speaks:

Let any one of you who is without sin be the first to throw a stone at her. (v 7)

With that, he's right back down writing on the ground, ignoring them. They slip away one by one. And then comes mercy. "Has no one condemned you?" he asks the woman. "No one, sir," she says, to which the Lord replies:

---

19 By "the Law," the Pharisees would have been referring to the Torah—what we call the Pentateuch, the first five books of the Bible. They were also referring to the law given within that Law: i.e. the set of laws given by God to his people, as we discussed in chapter 4.

> *Then neither do I condemn you ... Go now and leave your*
> *life of sin. (v 10-11)*

But wait—before we embrace Jesus' gentle mercy here (and it is gentle mercy), we have to ask about the law. According to the Old Testament, shouldn't this woman have been stoned? Why did Jesus, the Son of God, spare her? Did his merciful response imply that the Old Testament laws on adultery were bad, or wrong? Let's go back and find two important truths about the Old Testament law and its treatment of women involved in extramarital sex.

Responsible Together

Deuteronomy 22 v 13-30 is a key passage, offering a series of scenarios and related laws that help us make clear observations concerning women and extramarital sex. The first is that women and men were in general held equally responsible for the sin of extramarital sex. The woman was not exempt from responsibility, but neither was she held more responsible. She shared both the guilt and the punishment.

Deuteronomy 22 v 13-19, first, is all about protecting a wife falsely accused and slandered by her husband, who claims he found her not to be a virgin when he married her:

> *If a man takes a wife and, after sleeping with her, dislikes*
> *her and slanders her and gives her a bad name, saying, "I*
> *married this woman, but when I approached her, I did not*
> *find proof of her virginity," then the young woman's father*
> *and mother shall bring to the town elders at the gate proof*
> *that she was a virgin. Her father will say to the elders, "I*
> *gave my daughter in marriage to this man, but he dislikes*
> *her. Now he has slandered her and said, 'I did not find*

your daughter to be a virgin.' But here is the proof of my daughter's virginity." Then her parents shall display the cloth before the elders of the town, and the elders shall take the man and punish him. They shall fine him a hundred shekels of silver and give them to the young woman's father, because this man has given an Israelite virgin a bad name. She shall continue to be his wife; he must not divorce her as long as he lives.

The scenario is pretty complicated, and we won't go into the details; but the point is that the woman must be given an opportunity to prove her innocence (apparently by showing a cloth stained with the blood of her broken hymen, from her wedding night). With her innocence proven, she cannot be divorced or disgraced but must be cared for as a wife in her husband's house. We're looking into scenarios of sin here; the man in this case is perpetrating evil, slandering and mistreating his wife. The law names, reveals, and punishes his evil, while protecting his wife from it.

Those nine verses protecting a falsely accused wife are followed by two verses (v 20-21) condemning a guilty one—a wife who had indeed been falsely presented to her husband as a virgin, with no evidence to the contrary. She was to be stoned. (We'll go on without comment at this point, and come back to the nature of this severe judgment. First we need to hear the rest of the chapter, in order to take these verses in context.)

The very next verse (v 22) prescribes that, if a man is found sleeping with another man's wife, both the man and the woman must die. The difference between this scenario and the previous one is obviously that concrete evidence exists in this case against both the man and the woman. Both are present and guilty—and punished by death.

(Again, we will come back to the severity of the judgment—here, we need to notice the equality of the judgment). Without concrete evidence against a man, a woman
condemned by evidence was alone put to death. With evidence against both, the two shared the same guilt and the
same judgment.

The next section of Deuteronomy clarifies matters further, with another scenario of equally-shared guilt (v 23-24).
To understand, it helps to know that in that culture, a betrothed woman was not just engaged to be married in the
way we think of it; she was committed, as good as married. She was considered to be the man's wife. These two
verses picture a town scene in which a man sleeps with a
woman betrothed to another man. The implication is that
the sexual act was consensual; this is the point of noting
that the woman did not cry out. In a town with open-air
dwellings in close proximity, others would have been sure to
hear her if she had. She's guilty for agreeing, and he's guilty
for having "violated another man's wife" (v 24). They are
both to be stoned.

The Pharisees in John 8 were referring either to this
scenario or the previous one, depending on whether the
woman was betrothed or actually married. In either case,
the law stipulated that *both* the man and the woman were
to die. But as that woman is dragged before Jesus, the man
is... *nowhere to be seen.* Obviously, if she was indeed caught
in adultery, the man must have been caught there too. The
Pharisees were telling at best partial truth, both about
the incident and about the law. Their partial truth reveals
sexism—but only on their part, and not on God's.

Even as we are shocked by the severity of the punishment in Deuteronomy 22, we can see that the punishment
does not unfairly single out women. In the whole scope
of these laws, women participating in extramarital sex are

respected as equal partners in the sexual act, bearing not more but equal responsibility. We all know, however, that women too often are not equal partners, but forced sexually against their will. We must keep reading.

Protection for the Abused

We've seen various laws protecting women (women captured in battle; wives unjustly accused); Deuteronomy 22 v 25-29 deals with scenarios specifically involving sexual abuse. Here's our second observation: Old Testament law protected women in cases of sexual abuse. I wish I could sit down and talk this through with you as you are reading this. Both adultery and abuse are subjects that can rub hard against unhealed wounds, with deep hurt. If you know such wounds personally, I pray God's word will bring healing, not hurt, to your soul. I pray that even these hard Old Testament passages will reveal grace as you read them—the grace of our God, who has redeemed a people for himself through his beloved Son. It is his Son, our Lord Jesus, who best knows what it means to be shamed and publicly violated.

From the next scenario (v 25-27) emerges one of the strongest and, I think, most encouraging laws to be seen in relation to this subject. In contrast to the town setting, this sexual act takes place "out in the country," where no one would be able to hear a woman cry out for help. In this case, the betrothed woman is given the benefit of the doubt: she can be assumed to have cried out, when found and violated by a man. Most literally translated, the man in this case "seizes her and lies with her" (v 25, ESV); the NIV appropriately terms this "rape." Only the man is to be put to death. Verse 26 reiterates, "Do nothing to the woman; she has committed no sin deserving death." Verse 27 defends the woman further, acknowledging her plight: "Though the betrothed woman screamed, there was no one to rescue her." God sees and God steps in to defend.

Even in recent times and in many Western countries, it has often been difficult to prosecute a man who raped a woman, because female victims of rape have commonly been portrayed as seducers, guilty of inciting men to actions that in some way the women must have desired. So a guilty man could himself play the role of victim, rather than being convicted for the crime of rape against an unwilling woman. In some countries and cultures today, a female victim of rape is considered dishonored, and is even sometimes killed to protect the family's honor. It is good to find the Bible clear from the beginning in condemning the evil of rape, punishing men who do it, and protecting women who suffer the ravages of it.

The chapter's next (and even more challenging) scenario involves a man who rapes an unmarried virgin (v 28-29; see the similar passage in Exodus 22 v 16-17). *Another* scenario, you might say! If we don't regularly spend much time reading God's law in Exodus, Leviticus, Numbers, and Deuteronomy, we might be amazed at the detail of all these different scenarios in God's inspired revelation. But we should actually expect such detail, for the subject of sexual relations is obviously central and crucial to human experience. We human beings think about all these things in detail; how revealing and encouraging that God likewise pays so much attention, and tells us so.

The sexual union in these verses does not break an existing marriage bond; the solution offered is marriage. This case does not resolve all well for the woman: she evidently will be offered her rapist for a husband, who gets off by paying fifty shekels to her father (along with the lifelong obligation of marrying and caring for her). There are nuances here that offer a bit more light on the subject. Daniel Block suggests that the verb in Deuteronomy 22 v 29 ("he shall pay") could well be translated "may pay"—which would offer the woman's father a choice as to whether or not to accept this potential son-in-law.[20] As the extramarital sex in any case would make it difficult for this woman to be accepted by another husband, the required money and the security of marriage in themselves are meant as a help to the woman who has been violated, and who is viewed not as the guilty one but as the one to whom reparation must be made. At the least, the woman is covered by certain protections that are available to her and to her family.

All these Old Testament laws take place within a distorted patriarchal system. In a patriarchal system, the husband holds authority over his household. All sorts of practices grew up around patriarchy in ancient times: for example, a wife normally went to live in the household of her husband, and her role in bearing children to carry on her husband's line was crucial. Unmarried women were often unprotected and unrespected. Married women were often mistreated. Practices of polygamy developed. When we use the word "patriarchy" today, it's almost impossible to separate that word from all sorts of ungodly and sexist practices that have come to cling to it like barnacles to a seaside dock. In many contemporary contexts and cultures, lots of the barnacles still cling. The fulfillment of Genesis 3 v 16 is everywhere in evidence in this fallen world of sin. As Jesus said, the hearts of people are hard, and *it was not this way from the beginning* (Matthew 19 v 8).

Jesus knew the beginning of this story; he was there. And then he entered the story to save law-breakers.

---

20 *Deuteronomy* in the NIV Application Commentary series, pages 525-526.

Through the Old Testament law God was revealing himself. The law points relentlessly to the truths God established from creation: in particular, to the value of women and men alike as God's image-bearers, worthy of his attention, provision, and mercy. In a world full of sin and shame, laws such as the ones we've discussed served the merciful purpose of restraining sin, and protecting and providing for the most vulnerable in the midst of it. That would often be the women. Hence the existence of so many specific laws focused on protecting them from the abuse of men.

God Takes It Seriously

Even as we see that God treats women as equally responsible and protects women when abused, we still might have a good deal of trouble accepting the harshness of the punishment. Stoning? Death? For adultery? This is hard indeed. What is clear is that God views extramarital sex as a grievous evil, not to be tolerated among his people. This is evident from the refrain that comes after many of the scenarios in Deuteronomy 22, commanding the people to "purge the evil" from among them (v 21, 22, 24). Extramarital sex in God's eyes is evil, first and foremost because of God's established order in creation: one husband and one wife should become one flesh. Jesus makes clear not only that this is God's established order but also that to break it apart is an offense against God. It was Jesus, not some pastor or priest, who first said, "Therefore what God has joined together, let no one separate" (Matthew 19 v 6; Mark 10 v 9).

The sober details of the laws we have seen, including the shocking extremity of the penalties, tell us that in messing with God's establishment of sex within marriage, we're messing with the way he's set up his world to work. To reject his creation order is to reject our Creator personally—breaking apart what he himself created.

This is why sexual sin is just as grievous to God today as it was centuries ago. As with all sin, it brings sickness of soul—not only in agonizing cases of overt abuse but also in the more common and increasingly-accepted cases of disregard for God's design for sexual union within marriage. If we could see through to spiritual reality, we would probably tremble to contemplate the careless breaking apart of God's good and holy design for human sexuality. These breaks bleed death, although the wounds aren't always visible right now.

When a couple engages in sex outside of marriage, they often don't feel the impact of their sin in the moment, or sometimes even in a lifetime. Husbands or wives who commit adultery might feel satisfaction, or sometimes guilt, but not usually the heat of God's hatred for sexual sin as an evil to be purged. When women and men claim sexual independence, rejecting marriage bonds, they often don't realize the harm to their souls that comes with calling good what God calls evil. And those women and men include all of us; Jesus nailed every one of us when he explained that when we even look at another person lustfully, we have already committed adultery with that person in our heart (Matthew 5 v 27-28). All our hearts are broken.

It is hard for us sinners to see through to spiritual reality, especially in the midst of enjoying pleasure or power. Stoning is shocking; perhaps the shock of it helps open our eyes. God's word, by God's Spirit, does open our eyes to the sin that infects all of us—and by his grace we are drawn to bow in repentance before a holy God and find the mercy that he is always ready to extend. God is a God of justice, who holds the sexually unfaithful to account.

He is a God of compassion, who protects the vulnerable and abused. And he is a God of mercy, who forgives the guilty who turn to him for cleansing.

There's another aspect of the grievous evil of sexual sin: it infects not just one person but the community of God's people. God gave this Old Testament law to these offspring of Abraham in order to set them apart as his people. He had grown them into a great nation, just as he promised. He had redeemed them from Egypt. Now they were to live as his "treasured possession," a "kingdom of priests and a holy nation" (Exodus 19 v 5-6). These were the people through whose offspring God would bless the world, in the promised Christ. That offspring was not to be defiled.

Today, those who live in Christ are by faith part of that offspring, and we inherit that call to holiness—now with the purpose of together praising our God, who has redeemed us in Christ:

> *You are a chosen people, a royal priesthood, a holy nation,*
> *God's special possession, that you may declare the praises*
> *of him who called you out of darkness into his wonderful*
> *light. (1 Peter 2 v 9)*

Our holiness, including our sexual purity, is not just for our own good. We'll see in chapter 9 that marriage is a divinely-given picture of Christ and the church. The ultimate end for keeping marriage pure is that we his people might shine forth the glory of our Savior. God gives such stark prohibitions about the holiness of marriage in order to protect something beautiful and precious—a picture of his own Son.

Redeeming Gomer

In the end, sexual unfaithfulness reveals the unfaithfulness of our sinful hearts before God. Which brings us to a woman named Gomer, who lived in Israel in the 8th century BC (by this time, God's people were split between two kingdoms—the northern one called Israel, the southern one Judah). Gomer was a "promiscuous woman" whom God told the prophet Hosea to marry, in order to live out the story of God's mercy toward his unfaithful people. God's message through Hosea was that God's people were "like an adulterous wife … guilty of unfaithfulness to the LORD" (Hosea 1 v 2).

So Hosea the prophet married Gomer the promiscuous woman—it was a living parable. God told them to name their three children "God scatters," "Not loved," and "Not my people," showing God's impending punishment on his rebellious, idolatrous people (v 4-9). This is not a happy story. Gomer eventually left Hosea and their three children for another man.

And what did God tell Hosea to do?

> *Go, show our love to your wife again, though she is loved*
> *by another man and is an adulteress. Love her as the*
> *LORD loves the Israelites, though they turn to other gods.*
> *(Hosea 3 v 1)*

And so Hosea bought back his wife, paying the "bride-price" customarily paid to the family left behind by a woman when she married. This was a bride who had deserted her family; Hosea bought her back and took her home.

This is a picture of God; he tells us so. God promises to make a way for the people he called "Not loved" to be loved by him. To the people he called "Not my people," he will say, "You are my people," and they will say, "You are my God" (Hosea 2 v 23).

That's how merciful God is. I'm Gomer. You're Gomer. We're Gomer—spiritual adulterers. But from the beginning God had a plan to buy us back, and that plan has been accomplished. The God who loves us has redeemed us, bought us back, through the blood of Christ. We, his redeemed people, are pictured finally as Christ's bride, and we will one day be given "fine linen, bright and clean" to wear to our wedding (Revelation 19 v 7-8).

What is God like? Look at Jesus. Look again at Jesus standing before that woman caught in adultery. Jesus has mercy on her. He calls her to turn from her sin. He's come to redeem her from that sin, through his sacrifice on the cross on her behalf. She does deserve death. But that's not the whole story. Every woman and every man deserves death—the wages of our sin. But that's not the whole story. The hope of the Scriptures, for every woman and every man, is that Jesus came to offer us mercy. Through faith in his death on our behalf, we receive full forgiveness and new life with him. That is the whole story.

Women's Bodies

I have a good friend who is single and content in her soul. She and I both railed against our bodies as we ran the middle-age gauntlet of unpredictable emotions, sensations, and weight gain that often accompany the shut-down of the reproductive system. We shared many aspects of that experience, but I learned a lot as I heard her express the feeling that she was paying the price for goods she never got to take home. She felt the shut-down not only of body systems but also of dreams.

Then there's another friend, married and undergoing fertility treatment with her husband. When I asked her whether she might commit to speaking at an event a year away, she was frustrated in answering. Should she include a child in her plans for next year or not?

And then comes to mind my friend with six children— who has had to grapple in her own way with the workings of her reproductive system.

If you're reading this and you're a woman, I imagine you've expressed or heard expressed that sense that these bodies we've been given "just aren't fair." Why couldn't God have laid on the men some of the physical complications related to childbearing? Why do women bear the painful brunt of it?

If you are a woman who is not a mother, I hope you won't skip this chapter, because my aim is to ask what women's bodies, with all their distinctly female cycles and systems and stages, reveal about our Creator and the world he made. Is there any connection between the lofty truths of God's word and the issues we all discuss with our gynecologist in the little treatment room at the medical clinic?

After all, there's not just the pain of pregnancy and labor and birth, but there's the monthly discomfort—sometimes just bother, and sometimes various kinds of pain. Have you ever thought that the whole female reproductive system seems an unnecessarily laborious process? Couldn't it have been a system that you could activate and use only if and when you needed it? Couldn't it all have been neater, cleaner, and easier? Couldn't there have been a smoother progression from middle age to old age? And, yes, why do the men by comparison seem to dance through life, in regard to their bodies, which simply don't give them this kind of regular grief? What woman hasn't been jealous of men during a long hike with no rest-stop facilities?

If there is a connection of all this to spiritual reality, then we need to get hold of it, mainly so as to live in the love of God in the most comprehensive way, rather than with our fists raised toward heaven, or with inattention to the role of heaven in our earthly existence. I have found that, because women are necessarily connected to our bodily existence in the most regular and concrete ways, it means the world to women to think about how much God cares for our bodies. This is true in general of course for men as well; our human bodies are part of God's good creation, intended not just for this fallen world but also for the new heaven and earth to come. But it's women and our unique design that will be the focus here. Here's our question: *why did God design female bodies in a way that keeps on pestering us, so often in a manner that is physically or emotionally painful, with reminders of childbearing?*

This chapter is going to claim that women's bodies are living illustrations of God's truth: our bodies preach to us, we might say.

Answering Without Listening

As we listen to God's word, we begin to get the points our bodies are making. We begin to find true answers to our questions—answers desperately needed in a fallen world that, ever since Eden, echoes with voices that don't tell the truth. Before we aim to hear true answers, let's first acknowledge a host of untrue and unhelpful ones.

The female body has always been a mystery to be grappled with. Four centuries before Christ, the Greek philosopher Aristotle offered some very influential theories of reproduction. Aristotle's general claim was that a female is created when the course of nature that would produce a male somehow fails, and a female is born instead, sort of a male that didn't quite make it—or, as often translated, "as it were a defective male."[21] Variations of this view dominated the Western world for centuries.

Without the light of God's word, women and their bodies are often valued less than God intended. But they can also be valued more. In many religions throughout history, we find female goddesses whose power of fertility

---

21 See Book II of Aristotle's *On the Generation of Animals*. www2.ivcc.edu/gen2002/ Aristotle_Generation.htm. Selections originally from *The Oxford Translation of Aristotle. Vol. 5*. translated Arthur Platt, ed. W.D. Ross, (Clarendon Press, 1912). Accessed 6/20/17. For commentary on this, see Michael Nolan, "What Aquinas Never Said About Women," www.firstthings.com/article/1998/11/003-what- aquinas-never-said-about-women. Accessed 2/20/17.

is magnified and worshiped—as in the Roman goddess Venus (with her Greek counterpart Aphrodite). The
modern version of such worship appears in literature and
movements that encourage spirituality through female
connection to primal life, fertility, and even divinity. Just
search for some combination like "feminine and spirituality" on Amazon's website, for example, and you'll find
overwhelming evidence that we've not left behind goddess
worship today. The ability to conceive and carry new life is
a mystery no one denies; as a power separated from worship of our Creator, it can become a means of attempting
to raise oneself up to take his place.

For many of us the most pervasive (and therefore often
unnoticed) over-valuing of the female body comes in the
various media that constantly fill our vision with female
bodies and body parts. Walking through a mall or leafing
through a magazine is a kind of invitation to worship the
female form—and not just any female form, but the version valued for its beauty and sexual allure as defined by
the culture around us. Amazing, how those images can
float in virtual reality so perfectly free of bulges, wrinkles,
spots, or blemishes of any kind—as desirable and remote
as any goddess.

So our valuation of the female body can easily become
either much lower or much higher than God intended.
Of course, over-valuing the power or beauty of women's
bodies in the end undervalues women as whole beings created in God's image. Using women's bodies to sell things
cheapens those bodies more than we could ever measure.
Prostitution and pornography offer the most extreme and
devastating examples. Without listening to divine revelation, we quickly lose the proper value and glory of the
female body, designed along with the male body to reflect
the image of our Creator God.

As we consider our bodies in light of God's word, then, what do we see?

Our Bodies Preach Creation

The female body tells truths about God: first, about God our Creator. The Scriptures reveal that God, in his sovereign goodness, created his female image-bearers with bodies ready to conceive and bear new life. Even before the fall, Eve was designed with the capacity for childbearing (Genesis 1 v 28). The female body is distinct, made to complement the male body as a separate and beautiful creation of God—one that vividly reflects God's power to create life.

The original goodness of God's creation calls every woman to view her body, including its childbearing capacity, as good and as glorifying to our Creator. There's more to be said than this, of course—but we need to start with God's goodness, which shines through all he has made, broken and fallen as we are. God has embedded in women's bodies the ability to conceive and nurture new life; this is an amazing window for us, if we choose to look through it, on the God who made and sustains all life and who made us in his image. From the beginning and even after the fall, God mercifully ordained that human life should continue, and that women should play an intimate part in that process. In one sense, it's the men who are left out here, experiencing only a fleeting role; they might need a book on whether God is sexist in regard to them.

Can women who are not mothers celebrate this window on God that comes with their bodies? We've mentioned and we'll talk more about the way all women participate in the *pain* of the whole experience of childbearing, including its longings and losses. But I think that, in moments when by God's grace our souls are clearest, women also experience shared insight, and even wonder and thanksgiving to God, about things the "sisterhood" of females knows. Because women all experience life in similar bodies, we understand these mysteries in a very concrete way. All humans know the humbling fact that they came from the body of a woman; only women know what it is to have that body themselves.

Consider how remarkable it is that, with all the differences in shapes and sizes and colors of bodies, each unique, there remain recognizable systems of body parts and functions that are understood across time and place. We don't need translation to share basic understanding of a new baby, for example. On my first trip to Russia with my husband and our several-months-old baby, I didn't know the language at all but I soon noticed that, when I'd bring out the baby, in a social or a work setting, the women came round and came alive; the warmth and communication among us felt like cords with which someone had suddenly bound us all together. I got to know a number of those wonderful women; some of them had children and some of them did not. But they all reached out and connected—ministered to me, really—across the bridge of a baby. It was winter in Moscow, bitterly cold, and I learned from them, repeatedly, with no need for translation, that I did not wrap up my son tight enough or with enough blankets!

There were other bridges as well, with the women and the men; that was just one. Those women graciously and joyfully came across that bridge to me, and I'll never forget their warmth and welcome. Surely some of them carried inside them more painful stories than I knew. (And surely there were men around who loved babies, too!)

But there was (and there often can be, in my experience) a vivid moment of women coming together around the wonder of new life—sharing the wonder even in the midst of our different stories. Among Christian women, bound together by the Holy Spirit, the unity is even stronger; in the body of Christ we understand just how all the children belong to all of us. Their new life represents the next generation given by God to love and nurture and raise up to serve him. This is shared joy, in God's family. I've seen it. Even in the midst of pain—yes, I'm so aware that we need to talk about the pain.

How we share joy (and pain) in this process depends a great deal on our acknowledgment of the sovereign goodness of God in regard to childbearing. The One who created our bodies not only knows how they work; he directs their working. Do we really believe that? Do we even begin to grasp how everything that happens in this world happens through the sovereign hand of a Creator who sustains the sun and moon in their routes across the sky, and the eggs and sperm of a woman and man in their routes through human bodies?

When we look and listen, human bodies from their earliest stages preach God's sovereign, good creation. None of us is distanced from this truth: the Lord's sovereign goodness was at work when each of us was only a tiny being inside our mother's womb. As the psalmist considers this reality, he shows us how to respond to our Creator:

> *For you created my inmost being;*
> *you knit me together in my mother's womb.*
> *I praise you because I am fearfully and wonderfully made;*
> *your works are wonderful,*
> *I know that full well. (Psalm 139 v 13-14)*

Our Bodies Preach the Fall

Women's bodies preach truth about God our Creator—and about God our Judge. We heard God's declaration of the consequences of disobeying his word: to the woman would come first of all severe pains in childbearing: "painful labor" in giving birth to children, matched by the man's "painful toil" in working the earth (Genesis 3 v 16-17). They share the now-broken process of filling the earth and subduing it according to God's command.

Ever since, the whole childbearing-related process, with its various systems and stages, has been full of all kinds of pain. It is important for us to hear each other's stories of pain, especially those from women in stages different from ours. Those who've borne children need to hear the voices of sisters who have longed to do so and not been able. I see my world differently because I have heard the stories of single friends who watch the years and cycles of life go by, and who practice the discipline of embracing God's will; they have taught me much. I see my world differently because I have ached and prayed with friends through long months of fertility treatments that put great strain on a marriage, and that sometimes fail. I see my world differently because I've waited with friends who are hoping to adopt children, and in many cases joined in welcoming those children into the church family, but in other cases joined in grieving as adoptions fell through.

Of course into our minds immediately comes the pain of carrying and delivering a baby. It is impossible to summarize the intensity of a woman's labor pains, or the sharpness of the contrast between those moments (or hours) of agony and the very next moments of relief, when a child is delivered. Often-forgotten is some women's subsequent, ongoing pain. Very different is the piercing pain and grief of losing a baby, whether earlier or

later in a pregnancy. Often that pain is too little acknowl-
edged, deep as it is.

There are more kinds of pain than any one of us knows
in relation to female bodies. Millions of girls and women
around the globe know the inexpressible physical and
emotional pain of having their bodies sold and abused in
the sex-trafficking trade. The International Justice Mission
estimates 2 million children are being exploited globally, an
overwhelming majority of them girls:

> *"Human trafficking generates about $150 billion a year—*
> *two-thirds from commercial sexual exploitation."* [22]

This is deep pain, a deep perversion of God's good creation of human bodies, especially female ones. As the very
parts of female bodies designed to produce new life are
invaded with disease and death and hurt untold, girls and
women suffer on every level of their beings.

Sin has wreaked its havoc in this fallen world, and pain
spreads as a result. We might wonder: since pain related to
childbearing is a God-declared result of the fall, should we
be learning something from this pain? Many people today
focus on alleviating pain. In many parts of the world the
actual process of giving birth has become relatively mal-
leable, according to the amount of pain relief a woman
in labor chooses to receive. Most important, the mortality
rate of women and infants in childbirth is ever lower, due
to increasingly available medical interventions in cases of
emergency. And the ongoing general discomfort related to
female bodies' reproductive systems is often eased or even

---

22 International Justice Mission, *Sex Trafficking* in the IJM Casework Series: www.
ijm.org/sites/default/files/fact-sheets/IJM-Casework_Fact-Sheets_Sex-
Trafficking.pdf. Accessed 2/25/2017.

solved by drugs that lessen pain or manipulate reproductive cycles so they don't get in the way of our schedules and lifestyles.

Without commenting here on the morality of birth control, I will simply observe that it has played a major role in lifting the pain from the whole process of childbearing—especially if we include the pain of accepting an unwanted pregnancy. The other method most commonly used to avoid the pain of childbearing, abortion, deserves much more extensive comment than we have space for here. The extent of the wrong of killing a pre-born human life is found first in the violation of God's command not to murder (Exodus 20 v 13), and further in the wonder of that life God created. To end that life brings not relief but more kinds of pain associated with the weight of a fallen world. If you are reading this as someone who has been through this experience, I pray you will know not only that abortion is a sin against God, but also that God forgives all our sin when we come to him in repentance, trusting in Christ our Savior.

In one sense, we could say that modern medicine has blocked not just pain of various kinds, but also the opportunity to learn fully from the judgments God pronounced back in Genesis 3. Believe me, I'm not advocating for pain. I'm just wondering what God meant to show us through it, and whether we might still attempt to learn those lessons, in whatever pain God sovereignly allows for each of us. Because back in Eden God originally declared this pain and explained its cause, there's nowhere else to go than to him in dealing with it. Pain can and often does draw us back to God. Even those who don't know God, when they're suffering, often cry out—if not to him, then against him—asking why, and asking for help. God's word lights up the answer to such cries. It actually affirms our sighs and our cries, telling us that things are truly not as they were originally created. Listening to the Scriptures, we understand that the discomfort and pain that come from being a woman preach the fallenness of our world.

But they also point to our hope.

Our Bodies Preach Hope

In the Bible we discern a pattern—a pattern of unlikely births. It's a pattern of children born when the effects of the fall have been painfully evident. It's a pattern that points toward one child born of a most unlikely woman, a virgin. Female bodies preach creation. They preach the fall. And, finally and most wonderfully, they preach redemption.

God has always been directing the pattern of history from creation, even through the fall, and always for his redeeming purposes. And those purposes have been consistently and intricately tied up with childbirth. We heard the promise of offspring that God made to Eve, right after the fall. In Genesis 12 v 1-3 we hear another promise related to childbirth: God tells Abram that through his offspring all peoples on earth will be blessed. In Genesis 15 v 1-5, he's specifically promised a son. Now Abram and Sarai were old; she was not only past childbearing age, but she had lived a life of barrenness. Even when God renamed them Abraham ("Father of many") and Sarah ("Princess"—for her family would include kings), they still had no children. And yet that son, Isaac, was born, just as God had declared. God gives, and God withholds.

A woman named Hannah found that out. In 1 Samuel 1 v 5, we learn both that God "had closed [the] womb" of this godly woman, and that God answered her prayer for a child by opening it and allowing her to bear a son named Samuel, who became a great prophet, mightily used by God in establishing the kingdom of Israel. God was directing the course of redemptive history in these stories. He's always doing that in all our stories—all of them.

Just like Deborah sang after she saw God's hand at work, Hannah sings a song in 1 Samuel 2. Her song celebrates God's sovereign direction over both the high and the lowly—and she clearly sees herself as lowly. Maybe that's the key to grasping the truth of God's sovereign goodness. "The Lord brings death and makes alive," Hannah sings; "he brings down to the grave and raises up" (1 Samuel 2 v 6). Those words reach far ahead to another child who was born, who died, and who was raised up—all by God's hand.

And so our thoughts turn to Luke 1, where two more women sing because they see the sovereign hand of God both in their own wombs and in the course of redemptive history. They realize they're at the climax of that history: the virgin Mary, newly pregnant, is celebrating the coming of the promised Messiah, Abraham's seed, conceived in her by the Holy Spirit as the angel Gabriel had explained (Luke 1 v 26-38). Along with Mary's young voice comes Elizabeth's older one. Mary's relative Elizabeth, like Sarah centuries earlier, had been childless and past childbearing age. But again God opened a woman's womb. He gave Elizabeth and her husband Zechariah a son named John, who would grow up to announce to the world the coming of the Son of God.

Even in the womb, Elizabeth's son John began to announce Christ's coming, and his mother felt and proclaimed it. At the approach of Mary, Elizabeth's baby "leaped in her womb, and Elizabeth was filled with the Holy Spirit, crying out: 'Blessed are you among women, and blessed is the child you will bear!'" (Luke 1 v 42). How amazing that the good news of salvation for the world is so wound together with details of fertility and pregnancy and wombs. In his mercy, God ordained childbearing as the blessed means of his redeeming work in the world. Through the birth, death, and resurrection of his own Son, God redeemed us, bought us back, out of our sin and into restored relationship with him.

At the Heart of God's Eternal Plan

It's clearly not the case that only after the fall did God decide to incorporate childbirth into his redemptive plan. Speaking to believers, Paul explains that God "chose us in him [Christ] before the creation of the world" (Ephesians 1 v 4). God's plan from eternity included the sending of his Son into this world—his Son by whom this world was created (John 1 v 3; Colossians 1 v 16). That Jesus Christ should enter it affirms the goodness of this creation. Entering through the body of a woman, in the process of childbirth, he also participated in the painful judgment of this fallen creation: Jesus entered though blood and pain. All the judgment of sin Jesus embraced, took on himself, finally, at the cross. "God made him who had no sin to be sin for us, so that in him we might become the righteousness of God" (2 Corinthians 5 v 21). And so was fulfilled the promise of Genesis 3 v 15: that by the offspring of woman the serpent would be finally crushed.

Women and childbearing are at the heart of God's eternal plan of salvation. There's much discussion about the meaning of Paul's statement to Timothy that "women will be saved through childbearing—if they continue in faith, love and holiness with propriety" (1 Timothy 2 v 15). In the context of all of Scripture, we know the process of childbearing cannot be the effective means of salvation; childbearing itself is affected by the brokenness that salvation heals.

And whether or not a woman bears a child has nothing to do with her salvation, which comes through faith alone in Christ alone.

Mary the mother of Jesus wasn't saved through giving birth to Jesus. When on one occasion a woman called out to Jesus, "Blessed is the mother who gave you birth and nursed you," he replied, "Blessed rather are those who hear the word of God and obey it" (Luke 11 v 27, 28). That's what we see Mary doing, in Luke 1. Upon being presented with the mystery of conception through the power of the Holy Spirit, she responds with simple words of faith: "I am the Lord's servant ... May your word to me be fulfilled" (Luke 1 v 38). Mary heard God's word and obeyed it.

So what is Paul saying in 1 Timothy 2 v 15? It's certainly possible, as some suggest, that "childbearing" here specifi-cally points to the birth of Christ, who saves us. We noted earlier the context of this verse: 1 Timothy 2 v 13-14 refers to the creation and fall of Adam and Eve, and so we come to verse 15 with Genesis already on our minds; we naturally think back to God's promise concerning the offspring of a woman. I think it's also possible that "childbearing" in this verse is used to represent God's whole plan from the begin-ning as experienced distinctly by females: our creation with this defining capacity for childbirth; our pain surrounding childbirth as part of the consequences of the fall; our ul-timate hope in the Savior born. Women are called by God to embrace "childbearing," in this large sense—to receive God's whole word, which even our bodies preach.

Part of a Bigger Story

In God's word the truths of childbearing are lit up in all kinds of ways to reveal his redemptive plan. The Bible takes these physical truths and uses them to point to spiritual

reality. These truths are about more than themselves. Childbirth ultimately pictures new life in Christ—as when Jesus
talks about being "born again" (John 3 v 3), and Peter writes
of "new birth into a living hope" (1 Peter 1 v 3). Scripture's
many pictures include not only the wonder but also the
pain; Paul writes that the whole fallen creation is "groaning
as in the pains of childbirth right up to the present time"
(Romans 8 v 22). The judgment of God to come is vividly
described in terms of pregnancy: "While people are saying,
'Peace and safety,' destruction will come on them suddenly, as labor pains on a pregnant woman, and they will not
escape" (1 Thessalonians 5 v 3).

Most wonderful, I think, are the pictures given by the
prophet Isaiah of what it will be like to live with God forever as his redeemed people. Isaiah points toward a new
Jerusalem, a restored people—through the picture of a
nursing mother comforting her child. But in this picture
no woman is the mother—God is, and we, the "Jerusalem"
of God's people, are his eternally comforted children:

> I will extend peace to her [Jerusalem] like a river,
>   and the wealth of nations like a flooding stream;
> you will nurse and be carried on her arm
>   and dandled on her knees.
> As a mother comforts her child,
>   so will I comfort you. (Isaiah 66 v 12-13)

These pictures help us see what the Bible's story is all
about: God's plan of salvation that brings us back to himself, though his Son. Our bodies are part of this story, and
women's bodies preach this story—from creation, to the
fall, to the redemption that stretches out into eternity. Listening to this preaching, you can look at your body—all
that you have been given and all that you have not been

given—and offer your body in service to your Creator and Redeemer, knowing that his good hand is shaping every molecule and moment of your existence. You too can say, as Mary did, "I am the Lord's servant ... May your word to me be fulfilled" (Luke 1 v 38).

Well, is this all fair? The answer to that depends on how we view the story we're living in. If you see Jesus at the center of your story, then you know it's truly not fair— that the Lord Jesus should have come down into all this pain and taken it on himself, in order to take away our pain finally and fully and restore us to himself. We are part of an amazing story indeed. These bodies preach good news.

A Man Unlike
Any Other

I vividly remember a conversation from years ago, when I was just beginning to teach university students. Surrounded by thoughtful and challenging voices, I was in the process of examining my views on women and men and the church. This particular conversation was with a fellow teacher who had for years been part of the Christian world, and still was—even while she was asking a lot of questions about that world, especially questions related to women and women's rights. This woman was fun, smart, and challenging to talk with, and through her I considered more deeply than I had ever done before the ways in which women can be hurt through those who do not treat women as created equally with men in the image of God. This woman was one who had been hurt. She knew personally some of the reality of Genesis 3 v 16.

The moment I remember so well came in a conversation about Jesus. We were at a Christian conference together and had just heard what I thought was an encouraging talk from one of the Gospels. But my friend had not found it encouraging. Her only quiet comment was that the more she saw how women had been oppressed by men, especially in the church, the more she struggled to love Jesus—because he was a man.

Time to Look at Jesus

We've reached a crucial point in this book. It's time to look at Jesus the man, and to let him show us God. The disciple Philip asked Jesus to show his Father to his disciples—in effect, to let them see God. When Jesus responded, it was God speaking: "Don't you know me, Philip, even after I have been among you such a long time? Anyone who has seen me has seen the Father" (John 14 v 9). John explains this truth at the start of his Gospel: "No one has ever seen God, but the one and only Son, who is himself God and is in closest relationship with the Father, has made him known" (John 1 v 18).

These truths about Jesus mean that we can find certainty about the relationship between women and God by watching Jesus relate to women. We can be sure we'll be watching the God we've been seeing from Genesis 1 onwards—now in the flesh. It's hard to say this to women like the one who was finding it hard to love Jesus; her heart's hurt and her mind's views made it difficult for her to look at him. She bears the responsibility to open her eyes, but those who hurt her have put challenging obstacles in her line of vision. Knowing that in the end only God can open anybody's eyes, I (along with the believers around her) bear responsibility to keep asking God to turn her eyes towards his Son.

My goal in this chapter is simply for us to see and hear the Lord Jesus as he interacts with the women around him. Many have observed that Jesus overturned the sexist attitudes and practices that were commonplace in his day. We'll see this in the Gospel stories. But we'll also see that Jesus overturns the sexist attitudes and practices of any day—anything that would get in the way of bringing women and men into relationship with their Creator. Because Jesus is the way, the truth, and the life, no woman and no man can come to the Father except through him (John 14 v 6)—and he came inviting every woman and every man to come to the Father through him.

But first let's ask: Why did Jesus come as a *man*, talking about his *Father*? Why not a *woman*, talking about her *Mother*? God sometimes uses female imagery to show us himself, as in those verses we saw from Isaiah 66: "As a mother comforts her child, so will I comfort you; and you will be comforted over Jerusalem" (66 v 13). When Jesus came, he looked with sorrow on the city of Jerusalem, which was rejecting him, and lamented, "How often I have longed to gather your children together, as a hen gathers her chicks under her wings, and you were not willing" (Luke 13 v 34). These examples are comforting and revealing. God is clearly not male in the sense that a man is anatomically male; God is a being beyond gender, and he created both male and female to reflect his image.

But still, why come in the flesh as a man instead of a woman? From what we've seen so far in Scripture, we know it was not because men are by nature greater than women in value or goodness or giftedness; they're not. So why does God reveal *him*self as *Father, Son*, and Spirit? Why does the Bible's story take us from one *man*—Adam—to another *man*—Jesus Christ (see Romans 5 v 12-19)?

We can think of all sorts of practical and cultural reasons why "Father" and "Son" work better than "Mother" and "Daughter" ever could have. Throughout generations where, as a result of sin, men have "ruled" over women, a mother god and then a daughter in the flesh would not have been heeded or respected. But those sorts of reasons, even though they make some practical sense, don't really help. The Bible does not present God as taking on identities in order to relate to us, as he figures out in real time how to solve the world's problems. The Bible presents God as eternally God in three Persons. John 1 tells us that "the Word" was with God and was God from the beginning. It's that Word who was made flesh and dwelt among us: "the one and only Son, who came from the Father" (John 1 v 1-2, 14). When Jesus was born, he didn't become God's Son; rather, God's eternal Son became a man.

God didn't change himself to accommodate us; rather, he made us human beings to reflect him. That's what we saw in Genesis. We'll see further ramifications of this in the next chapters. At this point the focus is on God's Son, revealed to us as God in the flesh. My friend was refreshingly honest, actually, in facing not just her questions about the rights and roles of women but also her questions about Jesus. All these parts connect, and to receive the whole takes great humility and a submission to God's word—for all people, but for women in some unique ways. God is asking women to bow before a man—a man who is our Savior and Lord.

But that's not all there is to say. It's not just a matter of accepting what God's word says. It's also a matter of finding joy and refuge in what God says. I believe that, even though the friend I've been talking about was turning her back on Jesus because he was a man, if she had turned toward him she would have found huge comfort in knowing a man who is everything that all other men can never be. We're going to look into some stories from the Gospels that show how Jesus related to women. I hope these glimpses encourage you to see more clearly and love more deeply this Jesus, the Son who shows us the Father.

Known Fully and Fully Loved

In Jesus' encounters with a variety of women, often a single statement just seems to ring out from his lips. For example, when Jesus meets a woman at a well and strikes up a conversation, the climax of their discussion comes when she says she knows that the Messiah, the Christ, is coming, and Jesus responds, "I, the one speaking to you—I am he" (John 4 v 25-26). Throughout his earthly ministry until the very end, Jesus is guarded and slow to declare openly the fact that he is the promised Christ. This moment is almost shocking: he declares his identity right out—to, of all people, this *woman* from *Samaria*.

It is already shocking, in this story, that Jesus is speaking publicly with a woman; this was not an acceptable practice for men at that time. His disciples "were surprised to find him talking with a woman" (v 27). And this was not only a woman, but a Samaritan woman. Jews at that time despised Samaritans, who were ethnically only partly Jewish, and did not worship according to the Jewish law. The woman herself is shocked when Jesus asks her for a drink: "'You are a Jew and I am a Samaritan woman. How can you ask me for a drink?' (For Jews do not associate with Samaritans.)" (4 v 9).

Moreover, not only was this a Samaritan woman; this was a social outcast. She comes out alone for water in the uncomfortably hot middle of the day, probably to avoid meeting anyone. But she meets Jesus, and Jesus does not avoid difficult topics; he tells her he knows she's had five husbands and is living with a man who's not her husband (v 17-18). As all these details emerge, it's perhaps most surprising that Jesus moves into a pretty heavy theological discussion with this woman. She's not afraid to talk about spiritual things; she's interested and curious, and in response he hands her the truth. He tells her who he is. He lays this great gift of revelation that the prophets and wise religious leaders have been seeking and seeking, for centuries, right in the lap of this Samaritan woman. *Yes, I am the Messiah. I am he.*

Why did Jesus choose her? Well, the revelation of Messiah was less provocative in Samaria than in Judea, where such a direct claim could have precipitated his arrest by angry Jewish leaders too early in God's perfect timing. But why a woman, and this woman? Why is so much time taken speaking with her, and drawing out her embarrassing story of a sinful life? Why is it this outcast woman at the well to whom Jesus declares his identity and describes the living water he gives, that can well up in her to eternal life (v 13-14)?

This story doesn't explain Jesus' choice but it does show his heart. Jesus cared to know this individual woman, outcast as she was. He actually knew all about her. And he wanted to give her the living water of eternal life. She received it—in fact she ran and shared it with her whole town, many of whom also believed in Jesus (v 39-42). She was the first missionary to carry the message of Christ to a people group!

John devotes a lot of time to this story; we're meant to relish it. Picture it: Jesus looking this woman in the face and having this direct, weighty, compassionate conversation with her before finally telling her, "I am he." If his words are true, and if this story is true, then there is nothing my friend from years ago needed more—and nothing that any of us needs more—than to listen to Jesus.

Many people around us know many things about us, but none of them knows us fully. You may be sad about that—or you may feel glad to keep hidden some stories of how you've spoken, acted, or thought in the past.

You may fear the judgment or rejection of people whose opinion and affection you deeply value. This encounter of Jesus with the Samaritan woman should encourage us as we realize that Jesus sees each of us and knows us fully. The encouragement here comes not from an acceptance of our faults, but from the love of a Savior who came to bear the burden of those faults, to take our punishment, and to cleanse us from our sin. Here's our lasting encouragement: Jesus has made a way for us to enter the presence of the God of the universe (who sees into every heart). Through Christ the Messiah, as he explained to this woman, we can actually become the kind of worshipers God seeks: those who worship him "in the Spirit and in truth" (v 24).

Glimpses: Jesus and Women

As we watch Jesus encountering women, so many more statements ring out...

"Do you see this woman?" (Luke 7 v 44). That's what Jesus said to his Pharisee host, who scorned him for allowing a notoriously sinful woman to make a scene at the dinner table: weeping over Jesus' feet, wiping them with her hair, and pouring perfume on them from her alabaster jar. Simon the Pharisee saw only an undesirable, a woman who didn't measure up and whom you wouldn't want to touch you. Jesus saw a woman who greatly loved the one who could forgive her many sins. He told her that her sins were forgiven. He affirmed her believing heart: "Your faith has saved you; go in peace" (v 50). When others didn't, Jesus truly saw this woman.

"Your faith has healed you" (Luke 8 v 48). Jesus spoke such words not only to the woman anointing his feet; he spoke them also to a woman who, in the crush of a

crowd, just touched the edge of his cloak (v 42-48). This woman wanted to be healed from twelve years of bleeding—which, as we've seen, according to Old Testament laws would have made her unclean and excluded from fellowship and worship with God's people. She thought she could touch Jesus' cloak without being noticed. But, just as Jesus truly saw the woman anointing his feet, so Jesus truly saw this suffering woman, responded to her touch of faith, and healed both her body and her soul. Jesus calls this woman "daughter": "Daughter, your faith has healed you. Go in peace" (v 48).

The woman who suffers alone cannot go unnoticed by Jesus. He sees her, and he welcomes her into God's family as she puts her faith in him. You may be someone who has thought about Jesus, and even talked a lot about him, but who needs to take that step of simply and truly believing this: that Jesus the Son of God really exists, that he really is God, and that he sets his eye on you and sees your heart. If this is true, then it calls for a response: falling at his feet in faith and with thankfulness that he forgives your sins; he heals your heart. As you respond to the Lord Jesus, you know the joy of being received like a beloved daughter.

"Should not this woman, a daughter of Abraham ... be set free?" (Luke 13 v 16). Jesus heals another daughter—this time called "a daughter of Abraham," this time in the synagogue on the Sabbath (v 10-17). This woman is bent over, unable to stand up straight, having been "crippled by a spirit for eighteen years." When Jesus takes the unorthodox step of calling her forward from the back of the synagogue and putting his hands on her, "immediately she straightened up and praised God." The religious leaders condemn Jesus for healing on the Sabbath; Jesus responds to these "hypocrites"—who untie their ox or donkey to give them water

on the Sabbath—that he will free this woman from Satan's bonds on the Sabbath. This Jewish woman is part of their family (she is a descendant of Abraham); most importantly, this woman of faith is part of God's family. Again, Jesus stops everything to heal a woman and welcome her into the family of God.

We meet so many suffering women in these stories! And we meet so many women of faith, who make their way to the presence of Jesus—so many women seen, cared for, and healed by the Lord Jesus.

"Do you believe this?" (John 11 v 26). That's what Jesus asked Martha, in a private conversation with her after her brother Lazarus died. She had run outside to meet Jesus as he approached their house. As they stood together and spoke of the resurrection, Jesus gave to Martha those weighty words that have encouraged the church for centuries: "I am the resurrection and the life. Whoever believes in me, though he die, yet shall he live, and everyone who lives and believes in me shall never die" (v 25-26, ESV). But he didn't just give her a statement. He asked her a question: "Do you believe this?"

Jesus cares about the understanding and the faith of each individual follower of his, male or female. It was Martha whom he earlier rebuked for being "worried and upset about many things," when only one thing was needed (Luke 10 v 38-42). Jesus described that one thing as the "better" thing that Martha's sister Mary had chosen, on the occasion of their hosting Jesus (and probably a group of his followers) at their house. Martha was "distracted by all the preparations that had to be made," but Mary "sat at the Lord's feet listening to what he said."

Jesus' evident concern for these women to hear and believe his word was all the more striking at that time, for women were not allowed to handle and study the Scriptures

with the men. Jewish women participated in worship and
so were able to hear the word, but worship was segregated,
and for women formal study was off-limits. Jesus comes
along and teaches the women right along with the men.
He personally nurtures Martha in her faith, bringing her to
the point of looking back at Jesus and answering his question strongly and clearly: "Yes, Lord ... I believe that you
are the Messiah, the Son of God, who is to come into the
world" (John 11 v 27).

"Don't cry" (Luke 7 v 13). Again there is a crowd following Jesus, this time into the town of Nain, and again
he stops everything for a woman (v 11-17). This time it's
a widow, in a procession carrying out of the town gate
the dead body of her only son. Luke lets us see the compassion of our Savior: "When the Lord saw her, his heart
went out to her and he said, 'Don't cry'" (v 13). We read
not just that Jesus raised that son from the dead, but that
he "gave him back to his mother" (v 15).

Jesus noticed widows—too often the unnoticed and
left-out ones, both then and now. To illustrate faithful
and unceasing prayer, he told a parable about a wonderfully persistent widow (Luke 18 v 1-8). To reveal the
nature of true generosity towards God, he pointed out
a poor widow who, with her two small coins, gave more
than all those putting their rich gifts into the temple trea-
sury (Luke 21 v 1-4). As he died, Jesus ensured that his
own mother Mary would be cared for by his beloved disciple John (John 19 v 26-27). We must never miss how
much Jesus noticed the women around him. He noticed
not only their need and their hurt; he noticed and celebrated their faith.

"Go ... to my brothers and tell them" (John 20 v 17). Jesus
spoke these words to Mary Magdalene, commissioning a
woman to be the first witness to his resurrection. Mary

Magdalene was one of a whole group of women who followed Jesus and supported his ministry:

> *Jesus traveled about from one town and village to another,*
> *proclaiming the good news of the kingdom of God. The*
> *Twelve were with him, and also some women who had been*
> *cured of evil spirits and diseases: Mary (called Magdalene)*
> *from whom seven demons had come out; Joanna the wife of*
> *Chuza, the manager of Herod's household; Susanna; and*
> *many others. These women were helping to support him out*
> *of their own means. (Luke 8 v 1-3)*

The Gospels make clear what a crucial part women played in Jesus' ministry. Yes, the twelve disciples were men—and we'll talk about why. But along with those twelve are these named women and the "many others" who accompanied Jesus. They represent all socio-economic classes; perhaps some mentioned here were wealthy widows left with "their own means."

The women were there from start to finish. They were at the cross, when many others ran away in fear (Matthew 27 v 55-56). They watched the burial (Luke 23 v 55). It was Mary Magdalene who first went to the tomb on the first day of the week after Jesus' death, while it was still dark (John 20 v 1). And it was Mary Magdalene to whom Jesus first appeared and whom he commissioned to go and tell the disciples he was alive, even though at that time the law did not even allow women to bear witness in a court. From the time his mother Mary proclaimed praise to God for the child conceived in her to the time Mary Magdalene proclaimed the news of his resurrection from the dead, women were there, right at the heart of the most pivotal events in human history, announcing the events that light up eternity.

This Is Jesus

The strong words of writer Dorothy Sayers offer a great glimpse of Jesus in relation to women. In her essay *Are Women Human?* Sayers writes,

> *"Perhaps it is no wonder that the women were first at the Cradle and last at the Cross. They had never known a man like this Man—there had never been such another. A prophet and teacher who never nagged at them, who never flattered or coaxed or patronized; who never made arch jokes about them, never treated them either as 'The women, God help us!' or 'The ladies, God bless them!'; who rebuked without querulousness and praised without condescension; who took their questions and arguments seriously."* [23]

This man was unlike any other because he was fully man and fully God, the Son of God incarnate. Jesus shows us how God views women. In Jesus we see that God values women just as he values every human being—with all the grace and truth that emanate from the heart of God.

We should take care not to sentimentalize Jesus' relation to women. That's the brilliance of Dorothy Sayers' comments: she captures the way Jesus fully respected and challenged women as image-bearing human beings. In the end, what will keep us from sentimentality is not an affirmation of the value of women but a clear view of the person of Jesus. We need to see Jesus in his earthly ministry, as he welcomed and valued the human beings he came to save, and we need to see him in his heavenly ministry—as he is right now.

Jesus did what he came to earth to do: he died, bearing God's wrath for our sins, so that all who come to him like that weeping woman at his feet can be forgiven. He rose

---

23 *Are Women Human?* (Eerdmans, 1971), page 47.

from the grave, showing the full meaning of that declaration to Martha that he is the resurrection and the life.
And the great reality right now, even as you read this, is
that God has "raised Christ from the dead and seated him
at his right hand in the heavenly realms, far above all rule
and authority, power and dominion, and every name that
is invoked, not only in the present age but also in the one
to come" (Ephesians 1 v 20-21). In his vision of the risen
Christ in heaven, the apostle John saw…

> *… someone like a son of man, dressed in a robe reaching
> down to his feet and with a golden sash around his chest.
> The hair on his head was white like wool, as white as
> snow, and his eyes were like blazing fire. His feet were like
> bronze glowing in a furnace, and his voice was like
> the sound of rushing waters. In his right hand he held
> seven stars, and coming out of his mouth was a sharp,
> double-edged sword. His face was like the sun shining in
> all its brilliance. (Revelation 1 v 13-16)*

This is Jesus. This is the glorious One who came down
to show us the Father, so that we might come to the Father
through him. Jesus showed us God's glory by becoming a
man—a sinless man, who loves us and laid down his life
for us. This is the One we love, the One who at the cross
showed us how great is God's love for us. This is the One
we worship—a man unlike any other man: the Son of God
who sees and knows and listens and welcomes and heals
and saves. The love of Christ shining from the cross embraces each woman and each man alike who comes to him.
The love of the risen Christ shining from heaven pulls us
forward, in hope, toward the moment when we will see
him face to face. To whom else would you go?

Women and Marriage

In the last chapter we looked at women in relation to Jesus. Now we're looking at women in relation to marriage. It's not a far jump from one subject to the next. It seems farther, I think, when more time is spent teaching women how to be good wives than teaching women how to know Christ. As Paul speaks to wives and husbands in Ephesians 5, he stops and comments: "This is a profound mystery—but I am talking about Christ and the church" (Ephesians 5 v 32). Jesus taught that marriage is a temporary institution: "At the resurrection people will neither marry nor be given in marriage" (Matthew 22 v 30). Marriage is not eternal; it's crucial because it pictures something eternal—Christ and the church.

The Bible does give attention to roles within marriage, and so must we—as long as we, like the Bible, never cease to be talking about the Lord Jesus and his redeemed people. With that focus, our end goal will be not just happy marriages now but the spread of Christ's glory forever. And with that focus, this discussion becomes relevant and exciting not just for married Christians, but for all Christians.

Starting Head-On – Submission

The subject of male and female roles in marriage and the church has been dissected in detail by biblical scholars who are often categorized under two generally recognized labels: "complementarian" and "egalitarian."[24] This book would fit under the label "complementarian"—although I find labels increasingly unhelpful. Focusing on the Bible and its own words takes us to the heart of this topic. In general, challenging as it is, the goal for Christians must be for us to come to God's word (and keep coming to it) aiming to be shaped by it as we listen and learn, not to shape it according to any pre-packaged position.

A couple short chapters are not going to answer every question we may have! I will focus on Ephesians 5, since some of the Bible's clearest teaching on marriage comes in this letter sent to Ephesus that unfolds the beauty

---

24 A few examples may help. The "complementarian" position is offered with solid exposition by Claire Smith, in *God's Good Design: What the Bible Really Says about Men and Women* (Matthias Media, 2012). See also Andreas J. Kostenberger's *God, Marriage, and Family: Rebuilding the Biblical Foundation* (Crossway, 2004). The book Dr. Kostenberger edited with Thomas Schreiner offers a valuable critical and pastoral discussion: *Women in the Church: An Analysis and Application of 1 Timothy 2:9-15* (Crossway, 2016 (third edition)). One of the "classic" complementarian works is edited by John Piper and Wayne Grudem: *Recovering Biblical Manhood and Womanhood* (Crossway, 1991). Another older and still helpful volume is James B. Hurley's *Man and Woman in Biblical Perspective* (Wipf and Stock, 2002—originally published by Zondervan, 1981).

For a differing perspective, editor and contributor Gordon D. Fee (with general editors Ronald W. Pierce and Rebecca Merrill Groothuis) represents the "egalitarian" position clearly in *Biblical Equality: Complementarity without Hierarchy* (IVP Academic, 2005 (second edition)). For a more personal and revealing glimpse into the experience of those who have moved from complementarianism to egalitarianism, see *How I Changed My Mind about Women in Leadership,* ed. Alan F. Johnson (Zondervan, 2010).

An overview of some of the issues side by side can be found in *Two Views on Women in Ministry,* edited by Stanley N. Gundry (Zondervan, 2005 (revised edition)).

These books offer only a representative glimpse. In them can be found numerous valuable references to other authors and works.

and unity of Christ and his church. In this chapter Paul is calling the church to lives of Spirit-filled witness to Christ—and in 5 v 21 – 6 v 9 he brings this call home. His "household code" gives instruction for three relationships: wives and husbands; children and parents; and slaves and masters. The whole section begins with a main idea: "Submit to one another out of reverence for Christ" (5 v 21). How is this submission acted out? First, by wives to husbands:

> *Wives, submit yourselves to your own husbands as you do to the Lord. For the husband is the head of the wife as Christ is the head of the church, his body, of which he is the Savior. Now as the church submits to Christ, so also wives should submit to their husbands in everything.*
>
> *(v 22-24)*

To submit means literally *to put under*. It carries the meaning of subjecting oneself to the leadership or authority of another—here, the husband, who is the wife's "head." That word "head" can mean literally a head that sits on top of a body, or figuratively a person in authority, or a "source" (as in the source or head of a river). The most immediately evident meaning here, if a wife is called to *submit* to this head, is that the head carries authority *under which* the wife puts herself.

This meaning of "head" is confirmed first of all by a clear parallel drawn in this passage, between the context of marriage and that of the church. Paul sets two relationships (and two heads) side by side: the husband is the head of the wife as Christ is the head of the church. The idea of Christ as authoritative head has appeared already in Ephesians; we have seen 1 v 20-21 in the previous chapter of this book, and Paul then continues:

> *And God placed all things under his feet and appointed*
> *him to be head over everything for the church, which is his*
> *body, the fullness of him who fills everything in every way.*
> *(Ephesians 1 v 22-23)*

Christ is appointed by his Father to be head over everything for the church (which would then be under Christ's comprehensive authority). It's a stunningly big picture of Christ, and we get to be in it!

Back in Ephesians 5, the command to wives is expressed in terms of the parallel: as the church submits to Christ, so also wives should submit to their husbands. The temporary and visible relationship (husbands and wives) points to an eternal and presently invisible one (Christ and the church). The point of marriage becomes clear, as this parallel unfolds. Husbands and wives are not to aim just for good marriages. Their ultimate aim is to show the grand truth of a people loved by Christ our Redeemer, the head we forever obey and serve.

Paul again presents Christ as head and addresses roles of women and men, in an amazingly plain but profound verse, 1 Corinthians 11 v 3: "I want you to realize that the head of every man is Christ, and the head of the woman is man, and the head of Christ is God." This introduction to a quite complex passage shows at least one clear truth: there is an order to human relationships that reflects an order in the Godhead. Here we are told that Christ has a head: God his Father. Even though Christ is in very nature God, he submitted to his head, his Father: "For I have come down from heaven not to do my will but to do the will of him who sent me," Jesus said (John 6 v 38).

As the Father and Son relate through different roles, so husbands and wives created equally in God's image also relate through different roles, with the man called head.

This truth confirms the order we saw pervading the creation account in Genesis. In fact, Paul in this passage reaches back to that account for support: "For man did not come from woman, but woman from man; neither was man created for woman, but woman for man" (1 Corinthians 11 v 8-9). We'll come back to this passage. But what we're seeing so far are the basic truths that headship implies order and authority, and that headship is first and foremost found in God himself. God's creation reflects the Creator God.

And so we come back to wives, called to submit to their husbands as heads just as the church submits to Christ as its head. The marriage instructions of Ephesians 5 don't stop with verse 24. But even if they did, the command to wives would be quite clear, especially in light of the biblical context we've just glimpsed; a wife is called to put herself (not to be put, we should note, but to *put herself*) under the authoritative leadership of her husband.

Questions

I haven't met with many women to discuss Old Testament laws concerning battle captives—important as that subject is. But I have met with more than I can count who have questions about marriage and submission. How can we not have questions? *Can these verses really mean what they seem to mean? What on earth might this sort of submission actually look like? How can we possibly view it as beautiful or good?* These questions deeply affect our lives and those around us. These questions are some of the most important in the world—because they relate to so much more than just this world. In the rest of this chapter I will consider five questions I regularly find myself discussing.

Question One:

But isn't it true that in Christ there is no male or female (Galatians 3 v 28)? Doesn't that truth cancel the command for wives to submit? Isn't Paul claiming the gospel leaves the sexism of submission behind?

In Galatians 3 v 28, Paul is talking about unity in the body of Christ:

> *There is neither Jew nor Gentile, neither slave nor free,*
> *nor is there male and female, for you are all one in Christ*
> *Jesus.*

As people made alive through faith in Christ, we are one body connected to our head. We're all redeemed by his blood, and we together live in him. But that equality of life in Christ doesn't cancel out our differences: a female doesn't become not female, and a slave doesn't become not a slave. That's the beauty: even with differences, we are all equal in our value as created and redeemed human beings.

We saw that in 1 Corinthians 11 Paul affirms an order for men and women even from creation. But in the very same passage he also affirms the equality of men and women—in the Lord:

> *Nevertheless, in the Lord woman is not independent of*
> *man, nor is man independent of woman. For as woman*
> *came from man, so also man is born of woman. But every-*
> *thing comes from God. (1 Corinthians 11 v 11-12)*

Paul is not afraid to affirm relationships of both hierarchical order and equal value in God our Creator and Redeemer.

Some have suggested the introductory command in Ephesians 5 v 21 ("Submit to one another") is a call for everybody to submit to everybody else—flattening the order, so to speak. Indeed, every believer is called to submit to the rest, putting others' interests first, just as Christ did in becoming a servant. In Ephesians 5, however, this command unfolds through three sets of relationships in which one side is to submit to the other, with no reciprocity. Husbands are not told to submit to their wives, nor parents to children, nor masters to slaves. The ones in authority receive different commands, as we'll see. Although we're all to have the same servant-hearted humility, and although we're all equally loved by our Father, we're not all the same.

Question Two:

But what if my husband isn't like Christ? How can I submit to someone who isn't a good leader? If he were, I would. This doesn't seem fair.

We can't help but notice that Paul gives this submission command without much qualification. The husband is the head, says Paul—period. And wives are to submit to their husbands "in everything." This seems a lot to ask of a lot of wives of a lot of imperfect men.

It helps first of all to see what is commanded of husbands: that they be like Christ, who for love of the church laid down his life:

> *Husbands, love your wives, just as Christ loved the church and gave himself up for her to make her holy, cleansing her by the washing with water through the word, and to present her to himself as a radiant church, without stain or wrinkle or any other blemish, but holy and blameless. In this same way, husbands ought to love their wives as their own bodies. (Ephesians 5 v 25-28)*

The only thing harder than to submit to a head might be to be the head. How can a man ever live out the unfailing love of God for his people?

Here's where grace comes in. Because we live in Christ, Christ himself is living in us, granting us his resurrection power, through his Spirit; Paul's just been talking about being "filled with the Spirit" (v 18). We won't follow God's commands perfectly, either as ones who submit, or as ones submitted to. But the reality is that in spite of our sinful selves, we are called by God's grace to live out a picture of Christ and his church; the word tells us that's what God designed marriage to do.

Actually, this command to submit comes with a brief but crucial qualification. Wives are to submit to their husbands *as to the Lord* (v 22). This means that a wife's submission is not based on her husband's qualification for the role; her submission to Christ is primary, and submission to her husband reflects and flows from her relationship with Christ her Lord—this actually makes submission infinitely valuable and beautiful. Peter even commands wives to submit to husbands who are not believers, "so that, if any of them do not believe the word, they may be won over without words by the behavior of their wives, when they see the purity and reverence of your lives" (1 Peter 3 v 1-2). Marriage in the end is all about the gospel of the Lord Jesus.

To submit "as to the Lord" also means, however, that if a husband asks his wife to do something displeasing to the Lord, she will obey her Lord rather than her husband. If my husband asks me to lie or commit adultery, for example, I will not submit to him.

This means that I will not submit myself to abuse: that is, to a husband who uses his headship as an excuse for harm—perhaps physically, or sexually. Abuse can and does happen in many forms, and it represents a complete reversal of God's plan for marriage. Since the fall, it has been the case that men often rule harshly over women; abuse is part of the result of sin that Christ came to conquer. Christ points us to a redeemed way, the way of the cross. In light of his death and the power of his resurrection in us, a husband is called to reject the sin of harsh rule and instead to become a servant-leader. A wife likewise is called to reject a desire to contend and instead to submit to her husband's leadership. If this call goes unheeded by either spouse to the point of abuse, then the abused spouse must be given help by the church body of which she or he is a part.

It's absolutely crucial to remember that this passage in Ephesians comes in the context of instruction not to individuals but to the church. An abused spouse in a church body should never suffer alone. An abusive spouse in a church body should never be left alone. The leaders of a congregation have a responsibility to deal with not just doctrinal wrong but also moral wrong among their members. In the case of abuse, it is the responsibility of the church to address that abuse thoroughly, seeking the safety and well-being of church members and also involving civic authorities when laws have been broken.

The biblical model for marriage does not lead to abuse. Sin leads to abuse. Yes, the biblical model has been misused as an excuse for abuse, and some women have wrongly been told that the Bible teaches they must submit to abuse with no recourse. But it does not follow that sinful mishandling of biblical instruction makes the instruction itself evil and void. That would be like blaming and discarding the command to exercise hospitality because some hosts poison the food they serve their guests.

Ephesians 5 brings God's good call for husbands to lay down their lives for the good of their wives—and God's good call for wives to submit, as to the Lord. This is a call to live out a picture of God's grace to us in Christ. It's a gracious call. We answer it only by God's grace, and through it we show God's grace to a watching world.

Question Three:

But aren't these commands culturally bound and antiquated? Isn't Paul just reflecting the sexist society around him?

Here's where Genesis comes in. Paul does not base his argument on the cultural norms of his time. Paul's God-breathed words keep turning our gaze back: back to the foundations of creation that stretch out through all time and space. We saw one example in 1 Corinthians 11 v 8. Again in Ephesians 5, right after the instructions to husbands, Paul adds, "For this reason a man will leave his father and mother and be united to his wife, and the two will become one flesh" (v 31). Paul yanks this statement out of the creation story (just as we saw Jesus do) and plunks it down right in the middle of his marriage instructions to the church. He is saying that the fundamental model of marriage established back in Eden is a model that God meant, and means, to last. It gets stained and tarnished with sin. But it's nevertheless the model that stands, for from the beginning it was intended to show the mystery of Christ and his church.

Paul's instructions for husbands and wives wipe away all the fog from the window of marriage and let us see through to the reality of Christ and his church. This plan for marriage is not a culturally bound one; in fact, Paul's commands to husbands were revolutionary in the midst of a world where wives had no rights and were not generally treated with respect. The commands to love and to lay down one's life raise women from objects to be used to human beings to be treasured. They are gospel-saturated commands, and they are for the good of women.

That good has been borne out in culture after culture where men who meet Christ learn to act like Christ to their wives. In some cultures the change has been dramatic—as in Irian Jaya (Western New Guinea; now Papua, Indonesia). As I've visited that area, I've been amazed at the joyful communities of the many Christians there. But they will tell you stories of just a few generations ago when the people spread throughout many isolated villages worshiped false gods. The women suffered greatly: they were excluded from religious ceremonies, made to live off in huts by themselves, sometimes starved when there was food enough only for the men, and often grieving as a child would be taken for sacrifice to the gods. Today, many whole villages are Christian, and many men and women are learning the Scriptures and worshiping God together. The Christian faith has transformed their lives—especially those of the women and children.[25]

The Bible's vision for marriage is not culture-bound; it transforms sinful practices in every time and place—not yet perfectly. This is still a world full of sin. But Scripture's vision for marriage is long-term, stretching from creation to the day of Jesus' return. When he appears, the real picture will be fully focused, and Jesus the bridegroom will claim his bride, the church.

---

25 It has been a privilege to get to know Wes and Esther Dale, in the village of Mamit, Papua, Indonesia. (You still have to fly into this mountain-surrounded area, landing on a strip of gravel.) Wes' father, Stan, was among a group of Australian missionaries who introduced Christianity to some of the people groups in Papua. Stan Dale was killed and probably cannibalized by one of those groups; the story is told by Don Richardson in *Lords of the Earth* (Regal Books, 1977). Wes and his family have stayed there, teaching and translating the Bible and training pastors.

Question Four:

But do I have to be a doormat and never work outside the home and just raise kids and not have my own opinions about things? The job description for submission sounds simply sexist.

Consider the following report offered as fact by one woman who calls the teaching of headship and submission "baptized abuse" and "toxic theology":

> *"Biblical womanhood, headship, and male authority teaches women that they have no right to choose... well... anything. A trip to the mall is up to their husband, if he decides it's his business. If he determines that she needs to stay at home and homeschool her kids instead of teaching grad school with her Ph.D., then there is no discussion. She gets no say in the matter. If he decides that he wants to have sex, then her headache is of no consequence. If he decides that she needs to be thinner, then she goes on a diet. If he decides that she needs to wear makeup, then she goes to Sephora. None of this is considered abuse. It's considered the husband's God-given authority ...*
>
> *"Complementarianism means married women have no choice over their lives at all."* [26]

If this writer's description of biblical headship and submission were accurate, I would agree with her conclusion! Certainly there have been and are some who have contributed to this description by their actions and abuse. But you won't find anything like this description in the pages of Scripture.

One of the beauties of Scripture's instructions is that

---

26 Carol Howard Merritt, "Does Teaching Submission Encourage Abuse?" Christian Century (3/17/17), www.christiancentury.org/blog-post/does-teaching-submission-encourage-abuse. Accessed 3/24/17.

they don't prescribe practical details of headship and submission. This is troubling to those who want the Bible to
give precise rules for everything. It doesn't. And I'm glad
it doesn't. We shouldn't try to make it do so. Scripture has
a few words specifically for wives, and a few for husbands,
and it has thousands for every believer. This is why women
(and men) need to focus first and foremost on knowing
Christ. Women (and men) need to study and teach and live
on the whole Scriptures. Then it will follow more naturally for a wife to submit to her husband as to the Lord. It
will follow more naturally for a husband to love his wife
with Christ-like love. Our relationship with the Lord Jesus
Christ is primary and flows into every other relationship.
That's the point.

How does a wife pursue biblical submission to her husband as to the Lord? A friend of mine says that if we're
supposed to look like the church in relation to Christ, it's a
good idea to check and see how the church is called to relate
to him. Earlier in Ephesians 5, for example, Paul tells the
church at Ephesus to "find out what pleases the Lord" (v 10),
and to "understand what the Lord's will is" (v 17).

Thinking about those commands in the earlier verses
helps me understand submission in the later ones. Those
commands don't specify certain actions, but they com-
mend a heart attitude that seeks to understand and to
please. Such an attitude means respecting my husband's
will and sometimes bending my own will in response. It
means taking time to listen to my husband talk. It means
considering how to be the most suitable helper for the
one God has given to me to help. Some husbands might
like help packing their suitcases (mine doesn't); some like
help talking through teaching preparation (mine does).
Submission is something that happens deep inside, by
God's grace. It doesn't have anything to do with owning

or expressing opinions (sometimes different from my husband's); being a strong, thoughtful woman; or doing and deciding a whole lot of things by myself. It might have to do with learning about something or someone I would not otherwise be interested in. It might mean being willing to move to a place where I might not choose to live.

Depending on the unique factors in each marriage, one wife's help will look very different from another's. Even in various contexts, however, what will be similar is the heart attitude of respect that a submissive wife has for her husband and that flavors a home with a distinct and beautiful harmony.

It's not as if Scripture gives no concrete guidelines what-soever. For example, Scripture is clear that children are a gift from the Lord (Psalm 127 v 3) and so should be wel-comed in a marriage, should God choose to give them. God originally called for human beings to be fruitful and increase in number, filling the earth; generations of chil-dren are a part of his plan. The prophet Malachi preached to God's people about marital faithfulness and made chil-dren part of that message: "And what does the one God seek? Godly offspring" (Malachi 2 v 15). I won't draw any more conclusions here except to say that God evident-ly likes children! And in his infinite wisdom he designed women to be the ones to bear and nurture them in and with their own bodies.

Should God grant children, a wife is called to make a priority of loving and nurturing them, under her husband's leadership. Titus 2 tells us that older women are to "urge the younger women to love their husbands and children, to be self-controlled and pure, to be busy at home, to be kind, and to be subject to their husbands, so that no one will malign the word of God" (2 v 4-5). The priority of a woman's family is clear here. The call to godly character and hard work is also clear, including work at home but certainly not excluding work outside the home.

Actually, much of the work that is done outside the home today would have taken place in homes then. Priscilla (whom we'll meet later) might or might not have had children, but it's certain she and her husband together worked busily at home making tents, hosting guests and church gatherings, and discipling people (Acts 18 v 2-3, 26; Romans 16 v 3-5). Titus was pastoring in Crete, where apparently many people were unprincipled and lazy (Titus 1 v 12)—surely including the women. There is a beautifully active, outward focus in this book's commands to the various parts of the church: the motivation for the wives is "so that no one will malign the word of God" (2 v 5). "Home" then becomes a springboard for gospel witness, rather than a retreat or an all-consuming occupation.

Wives live out these truths of Christ in all sorts of ways—ways that squash the stereotypes of submission. I once published an article on The Gospel Coalition website that included the voices of married women committed to the Bible's teaching on headship and submission.[27] These were strong, gifted, active, godly women. They were bearing witness to the ways in which their husbands lovingly encouraged and supported them in developing their gifts. Good examples abound in the church; these stories need to be told. But many of the comments entered on the blog were skeptical, saying in effect, "Come on—this can't be real! We know that wives who submit to their husbands can't really live such full, rich lives!" But it was, and is, real. Wives committed to these biblical teachings know a fullness we can't measure, because they are living out a reality much greater

27 "Wives Speak Out," www.thegospelcoalition.org/article/wives-speak-out (11/22/11). Accessed 3/23/2017.

than their own marriage; they are a living picture of Christ and his church.

Question Five:
But I'm single. How does all this apply to me?

In a myriad of ways. For one thing, every believer needs to understand these truths in order to teach them and speak rightly of them; all of us are responsible for raising up the next generation of believers. The church will be strengthened by a chorus of diverse voices bearing witness to the goodness of God's revelation concerning marriage, speaking clearly and winsomely in a world that increasingly contradicts God's word at every turn. These are not truths to hide. They are truths to celebrate, because they are all about the Lord Jesus.

Through family and friends, all of us know both sorrow and joy in relation to marriage. Only by the light of the Spirit-inspired word can we process the painful ways in which God's plan for marriage gets broken, or can we truly rejoice when we see Christ and the church clearly pictured by a husband and wife. Only according to this word can we encourage and pray rightly for the marriages of those around us.

Hebrews 13 v 4 says, "Marriage should be honored by all, and the marriage bed kept pure." This verse speaks to every believer. It means, for a start, that I as a woman will not seek intimate interaction of any kind with a man who is someone else's husband, or perhaps someone else's future husband. This is a gracious warning, helping all of us guard against impurity in our relationships. Ultimately, such warnings help strengthen the church and clarify the picture of Christ we show to each other and the world around us. If Ephesians 5 is true, then honoring marriage brings honor to Christ and the church.

Longing for Him

Finally, seeing marriage as a picture of Christ and the church makes us long for his appearing. This longing seems to grow the longer a person is either married or not married. Even in the best marriages there is inevitably the sense of imperfection, the moments of failing, the grief when one loses a spouse. Even the joys of marriage are infused with longing for the ultimate, eternal Giver of joy. In struggling marriages, where the window on Christ and the church is very, very foggy and life can be very, very hard, the need for our perfect head becomes agonizingly clear and the church's future becomes increasingly precious. And in the single life, a person longs for a companion, for intimacy, for a shared ordinary loving presence… for all that is ultimately satisfied in the Lord Jesus Christ. Some single friends seem to me to have a distinctively focused joy in and longing for Christ; they have learned to commune deeply with the only One who can satisfy our deepest human needs.

To think on the mystery of marriage and how it shows us Christ and the church makes all of us long to see our Redeemer face to face. For followers of Jesus Christ, marriage from any angle makes us long for his appearing.

Women and the Church

W e've arrived at the church. We've been reaching into it all along, but we're finally fully here. I find that women often begin discussion about women and God with the church—because this is where we live, or aim to live, in real-life relationships with other believers. Maybe you're a woman who's serving happily in a local congregation. Maybe you're just considering getting involved. Maybe you're in the midst of heated discussions about gender roles in your church. Maybe you love your church and want to serve, but you're having a hard time figuring out how. Maybe you've been hurt by a church, or you're feeling like those rules excluding women from being pastors and elders are just not fair. (Maybe you sit through sermons and secretly think you could do a better job.)

In a book that affirms God's goodness to women, we've got to address the church. The church is the remarkable resolution to the Bible's story.

The Place of the Church in the Story

Perhaps the most important thing about this chapter is that it builds on all the previous ones, starting with chapter 1 on Genesis 1. The whole rest of the story confirms God's purpose for the human beings he created: unity in true worship of him. Jesus came to lay down his life to accomplish that purpose. Marriage pictures it. All of us who live in him get to live out that purpose both now and into eternity, as the bride of Christ—as the church.

What is the church? Sometimes when we talk about the church in relation to issues like women's and men's roles, we tend to think of it as an organization where we have to find our place for a time—like a business where people are employed. The Bible, however, pictures the church as a living organism: Christ's body connected to Christ our head (Colossians 1 v 18; Ephesians 5 v 23); a spiritual house of living stones with Jesus as the cornerstone (1 Peter 2 v 4-6); and, as we saw last chapter, Christ's bride, loving him as our bridegroom (Luke 5 v 33-35; Ephesians 5 v 25-33). Such pictures light up the story in which we get to live as the people of God. If we're believers, our identity changes forever, and we are part of this eternally redeemed people called "the church."

Sometimes (not always, and not in this book) a capital letter shows we're talking about the universal "Church": God's people in all places and times. The universal church is an invisible fellowship of believers that will become visible and complete when Jesus returns. Until then, we live in various outposts of that church: local congregations that comprise the present visible church, following God's word and called to make disciples in all nations. After the Gospels, every New Testament book speaks into the context of local churches. These churches represent our identity in Christ: the church is who we are. For Christian women, then, the question is not whether we can find a place in the church. The question is how we should live out our place in the body of Christ—and how men and women in our churches can together show Christ to the world.

We've seen that in his earthly life Jesus showed full and equal respect for the women and men around him. This same Jesus as head of his church does the same. God sent his Son to restore men and women to relationship with him and with each other. The full picture of that restoration bursts into view in the church, as men and women become one in Christ. This is the restoration that will last forever. As believers, we get to live in it now.

Living It Out

How, then, are women to live out their God-given place in Christ's body, the church? One good way to answer this question is to look at examples and descriptions of women mentioned in the New Testament epistles, the Spirit-inspired letters written by apostles to various churches and pastors. Too often, we start with getting clear on what these epistles do not permit women to do, and then we briefly acknowledge what women can do. Let's start with *what we see women doing.* In the process, we'll not only see the boundaries and how they make sense; we'll see the whole landscape and how it is beautiful.

The landscape of the church is beautiful because it includes a diversity of human beings, male and female, young and old, together making up Christ's body. Even as we focus on words directly relating to women, it's important to keep remembering that the New Testament is most full of teaching and encouragements that apply to men and women alike. It is good to picture the whole church together receiving commands like Paul's to let the word dwell in us richly, "as you teach and admonish one another with all wisdom through psalms, hymns, and songs from the Spirit, singing to God with gratitude in your hearts" (Colossians 3 v 16).

Praying and Prophesying

Let's return to 1 Corinthians 11, where we saw Paul begin by showing an order between woman and man that reflects the order between Christ and God. That's the main principle of this section, in which Paul is addressing worship practices, one of his areas of instruction for the church in Corinth. Paul's central point is that the creational distinctions between men and women should be respected and affirmed in worship. He applies his point to the Corinthians with reference to head-coverings and length of hair, which carried specific meanings for men and women in that society. A married woman, for example, was expected to cover her head—to show that she was married. A head-covering was a sign of identity and respect for her husband-head.[28]

But in the process of noticing order and distinction between men and women, we shouldn't miss what the men and women are doing:

> *Every man who prays or prophesies with his head covered dishonors his head. But every woman who prays or prophesies with her head uncovered dishonors her head— it is the same as having her head shaved ... Judge for yourselves: Is it proper for a woman to pray to God with her head uncovered? (v 4-5, 13)*

The clear assumption here is that both men and women will participate in public worship through prayer and prophecy.

We know how to define prayer—direct communion with God in praise and petition, made possible by the Lord Jesus,

---

28 One of the best and more detailed discussions of 1 Corinthians 11 v 1-66 is found in Claire Smith's *God's Good Design: What the Bible Really Says about Men and Women* (Matthias Media, 2012), pages 53-80.

whose blood cleanses us and gives us access to his Father in his name. The picture here is of men and women worshiping together in prayer as men and women. It's a picture that shows fulfillment of God's original purpose in creating male and female in his image: in prayer, members of this church are reflecting the triune God together as one body, in unbroken relationship with him and with each other.

But what about *prophecy*? We saw Deborah prophesying in the Old Testament. Is Paul talking about the same activity? Probably not exactly. In Old Testament times, prophets delivered God's inspired word, writing it down as they were carried along by the Holy Spirit (2 Peter 1 v 21). In New Testament times, the apostles delivered God's inspired word, writing it down as they were carried along by the Holy Spirit, and bringing to completion God's written revelation. (False prophets exist as well, in all times; they deliver words that are not from God.) In the church established upon God's completed Scriptures, words of prophecy are not the same as God's inspired word; according to Paul's teaching we now understand prophecy as prompted by the Holy Spirit and delivered in a church congregation, but subject to evaluation and correction by the Scriptures, under the oversight of elders who judge according to the apostolic or biblical witness.[29]

Paul gives careful instruction as to how prophecies should be offered in an orderly way in the gathered church, one by one, so that all can benefit (1 Corinthians 14 v 26-40). Women would have taken full part in the offering of prophecy, among those who brought "a hymn, a word of instruction, a revelation, a tongue or an interpretation" (v 26). Imagine the variety of voices participating in the

---

29 John Piper gives a clear and succinct explanation of New Testament prophecy: www.desiringgod.org/articles/the-new-testament-gift-of-prophecy. Accessed 10/9/17.

times of worship. This is important, and it is beautiful. In a recent Sunday morning worship service I attended, a woman gave a moving testimony about adoption. It included a bit of her personal story and some biblical exhortations based on God's adoption of us into his family. It was a good word—and an example of something I would call New Testament "prophecy."

Paul goes on to talk about the judgment of prophecies (v 29-33)—and it's in this context that he gives his controversial instruction that women are to be silent:

> *Women should remain silent in the churches. They are not allowed to speak, but must be in submission, as the law says. If they want to inquire about something, they should ask their own husbands at home; for it is disgraceful for a woman to speak in the church. (v 34-35)*

We've just seen women praying and prophesying—so this is obviously not a call to utter silence. Nevertheless, during evaluation of the prophecies, women were to be silent. Paul focuses in on wives who, instead of speaking during this judgment process, can honor their husbands by waiting and discussing later with them at home.

Paul also explains why order is important. That phrase "as the law says" (14 v 34) probably refers again to Genesis and the ordered creation of man and woman in the books of Moses—called "the law." The fundamental reason lies in the nature of God: "For God is not a God of disorder but of peace" (v 33). The Godhead exists in perfect, ordered relationship—and men and women reflect that order (11 v 3). That order is clearly meant to shine forth in the church, even as men and women participate together in prayer and prophecy.

Teaching and Learning

Women are also called to learn and to teach. The example of Priscilla has encouraged many, including me. We've noted that Priscilla shared both tentmaking and gospel teaching with her husband, Aquila (Acts 18 v 1-3, 18-26). The two are always mentioned together, three times with Priscilla's name first, and three times with Aquila's name first. That pleasing balance seems to represent their partnership in life and ministry, with Priscilla as a full partner. Paul, also a tent-maker, lived and worked with them in Corinth, and surely taught them much during their hours together. Priscilla and Aquila hosted a church in their house, but they both also traveled with Paul, who reports of them that "They risked their lives for me" (Romans 16 v 4-5).

Perhaps the most beautiful detailed report of this couple comes from their interaction with Apollos, an eloquent speaker who was teaching about Jesus but didn't understand the whole truth of the gospel. Aquila and Priscilla heard him and then acted with an exemplary combination of graciousness and concern for truth: "They invited him to their home and explained to him the way of God more adequately" (Acts 18 v 26).

Well, you might be saying, Priscilla still wasn't a formal teacher; she just taught along with her husband, informally. In response I'd say first that we should never underestimate the power of such ministry. Mixed with hospitality and humility, Priscilla's and Aquila's teaching obviously made its way into a huge number of lives, including that of one of the most influential preachers of the day.

The women's teaching mentioned in Titus 2 also sounds like it might often involve informal settings and personal relationships. Titus is to teach older women to live reverent lives themselves and to "teach what is good" to younger women (Titus 2 v 3), with an emphasis on family relationships, as we have seen. In the context of that letter, which urges the intertwining of sound doctrine and good deeds in the church, we can assume that older women would be teaching "what is good" by instructing younger women in both good doctrine *and* good works. Again, this crucial ministry among women is not to be taken lightly. We are all teachers in a variety of ways, whether from podiums before crowds or at bedsides of children or around kitchen tables with friends.

Second, though, I'd say you are right: in the Scriptures, women are nowhere encouraged to be formal teachers of the church the way Paul encourages Timothy or Titus in the pastoral epistles. In fact, Paul addresses this issue with Pastor Timothy in one of the most debated verses of the New Testament, 1 Timothy 2 v 12: "I do not permit a woman to teach or to exercise authority over a man; rather, she is to remain quiet" (ESV). Books have been written on this verse, as mentioned in the last chapter (see footnote no. 24). As we briefly discuss it, the first important point is that the preceding verse says a woman should learn: "A woman should learn in quietness and full submission" (v 11). Again we see an encouragement of women's growth and participation, and again within a definite order. The picture of Mary sitting at the feet of Jesus might come to mind.

But here's that word "submission" again. This time it comes in the context of a letter to a pastor about the church. Paul is writing "so that ... you will know how people ought to conduct themselves in God's household, which is the church of the living God" (3 v 14-15). In 2 v 8-10, Paul's just been addressing the behavior of men and women in the fellowship of worshipers. In this context, then, verse 11 is speaking of women submitting to the "overseers" or "elders" of the church—whom Paul goes on to discuss in the very next chapter of the letter.

In both 1 Timothy and Titus, Paul specifically describes the qualifications of men called to lead the church: these "overseers" must be strong in godly character, faithful leaders of their families, *and* "able to teach" (1 Timothy 3 v 2), ready to "encourage others by sound doctrine and refute those who oppose it" (Titus 1 v 9). It is men so qualified who are to lead the church in expounding the Scriptures, judging prophecies, and so on. This is an authoritative role to which the whole congregation submits just as a wife submits to her husband. The fact that God is a God of order is patterned into all the layers of the world he created, surely ultimately so that we would all learn to submit to him as our sovereign Lord God.

So 1 Timothy 2 v 11 addresses what women *should* do, and verse 12 what they should *not*: teach or exercise authority over a man. Of course, both men and women are to submit to the elders; but these instructions are specifically for women. It has been conjectured that the women in the church at Ephesus were being especially disruptive, or perhaps grasping for authority in ungodly ways. The text does not say that. For immediate support Paul goes not to the cultural context, but to Genesis and the order of creation: "For Adam was formed first, then Eve. And Adam was not the one deceived; it was the woman who was deceived and became a sinner" (v 13-14).

Through the logic of these verses, Paul bases his order of authority within the church directly on God's original creation order. Just as the New Testament's teaching on headship in marriage takes us back to Genesis (see chapter 9), so does its teaching on church order. The argument of this section in 1 Timothy 2 appears to progress like this: women should not have this certain kind of role associated with the overseers/elders of a church, because ("For," v 13) this kind of authority was invested in the man at creation when he was made first. The man was given God's word to live by, and then held responsible by God for guarding that word above all else.

This leads us to the point of Paul's noting that Adam was not deceived, but rather the woman. Adam was the one held responsible by God not just for eating the fruit, but for listening to his wife (Genesis 3 v 17). The point is that he abdicated his responsibility to guard God's word— he ate the fruit his wife gave him while fully aware that he was disobeying God's command. These words in 1 Timothy 2 have nothing to do with concluding that all women are more easily deceived than all men just because Eve was deceived; they are about men being held responsible to guard God's word and lead a community (of two, or two hundred, or two thousand) where that word is followed.

This creational truth explains the historical fabric of leadership among God's people. In the Old Testament, priests were to be qualified males, according to God's law (Exodus 29 v 30). Jesus chose male disciples (Mark 3 v 13-19). And now the leaders of his church are to be qualified males.

The Principles and the Practice

How do we process this Genesis-based instruction that a woman must not teach or exercise authority over a man? What are the implications for women? Stepping back and listening again, we note the call to quietness that begins and ends 1 Timothy 2 v 11 and 12; this must be important. It points to the heart as well as to the tongue. Verse 12 specifies certain areas in which women should particularly practice quietness—certain authoritative roles of overseers that are not permitted for women—and according to the context we can summarize them this way: teaching the

Scriptures in the gathered assembly of God's worshiping people (as in the Bible teaching done by pastors and elders in regular church services); and exercising authority over the congregation (as in the spiritual authority that pastors and elders have, to judge doctrines and prophecies, conduct church discipline, and so on).[30]

Verses 13-15 are crucial to understanding this passage: first because, as we've seen, they point us back to Genesis, in which God's original order was established and then disrupted by sin; second because they remind us of God's overarching plan from the start, as verse 15 concludes by echoing Genesis 3's promise of an offspring: "But women will be saved through childbearing—if they continue in faith, love and holiness with propriety." The whole challenging passage lands on this strange, beautiful verse that ultimately turns women to Christ the Savior and the hope found in him (see pages 121-122). The word "continue" urges us forward: Paul is encouraging women to press ahead faithfully, increasingly showing God's image as his

---

30 Even among those who agree this verse teaches male church leadership, there is disagreement about the meaning of "or"; see the books recommended in chapter 9 (footnote no. 24) for in-depth discussion. The specific issue is whether the "or" (Greek *oude*) creates what's called a "hendiadys," blending into one meaning the two words it joins, so that the verse would address not two things but only one: something like "authoritative teaching." One possible implication of this position is that women are permitted to teach in the gathered worshiping church, as long as they don't do it holding in themselves the authority of elders, but rather speaking under that authority. James Hurley accepts these words as a hendiadys, as does Kathy Keller: see Hurley's *Man and Woman in Biblical Perspective*, page 201; and Keller's *Jesus, Justice, and Gender Roles: A Case for Gender Roles in Ministry* (Zondervan, 2012, ebook location 205 of 684).

However, Claire Smith, Andreas Kostenberger, and Douglas Moo among others have argued quite convincingly that the *oude* here joins two related but distinct things: teaching, and exercising authority (see especially Kostenberger's chapter 3, "A Complex Sentence: The Syntax of 1 Timothy 2:12," in *Women in the Church: An Analysis and Application of 1 Timothy 2:9-15*, pages 117-161; and Moo's chapter, "What Does It Mean Not to Teach or Have Authority Over Men?" in *Recovering Biblical Manhood and Womanhood*, ed. John Piper and Wayne Grudem, pages 179-193).

female image-bearers until the salvation story is complete. This is a good, strong word for women.

This pressing ahead happens in the local church context, and the process is complex. Individual church congregations that affirm Scripture's basic teaching of male leadership must work out under the guidance of their own pastors and elders how to apply these principles in the many gray areas of church life—such as whether a woman should lead or co-lead a small-group Bible study of mixed adult members; whether a woman should teach a church class (or which church classes) of mixed adult members; how and when a woman should participate in regular church services, and so forth. We're tempted to desire explicit lists of dos and don'ts; but, just as we noted in regard to marriage, in regard to church order the Bible does not give details about specific situations. It is the elders' role to lead congregations in faithfully following the word, teaching and explaining as clearly as possible their position in these areas. It is the role of church members, both women and men, to embrace that leadership joyfully and prayerfully. And it is surely the role of all of us to speak and act with charity toward brothers and sisters who differ in the working out of these teachings.

But let's remember: this specific instruction of Paul comes in the context of Scripture's clear encouragement of women to teach. It is crucial to reiterate that 1 Timothy 2 v 12, which guards the role of elder/pastor for qualified men, does not address and therefore does not limit the many sorts of speaking and teaching women ought to be encouraged to do, according to their maturity and their gifts. In regard to competency, women are no different from men in their ability to excel as teachers. Those who affirm this order given in God's word should be the *most* free and happy to urge women to serve and teach in every way possible within this good order. It is important and beautiful to see women participating in the life and worship of the church in all kinds of ways, including teaching; in fact, when women are actively and visibly participating, the church is better able to celebrate the reality of unity in God's image as he intended it way back in Genesis 1.

All Kinds of Things

I think Romans 16 is one of the most beautiful chapters in the New Testament. It's not about women; it's about the church. As he sends personal greetings and commendations at the end of this magnificent epistle, Paul addresses a whole cast of women and men, all wonderfully mixed up together. In the process, he reveals a spectrum of ways in which these believers are serving the Lord side by side. Women were not passive helpers in church life; they were praying and prophesying and learning and teaching. Like Euodia and Syntyche in Philippi, they "contended at [Paul's] side in the cause of the gospel" (Philippians 4 v 3).

In Romans 16, first comes Phoebe, "a deacon of the church in Cenchreae" (v 1). She was probably the one who carried this epistle to the Romans; Paul asks them to "receive her in the Lord in a way worthy of his people and to give her any help she may need from you, for she has been the benefactor of many people, including me" (v 2).

There's debate about Phoebe, because the word "deacon" is the Greek word *diakonos*, which can mean either "servant" or "deacon"—it is used both ways in various passages. We won't solve here the question of whether women should hold the office of deacon—an office of service to the church involving care for physical needs. For our purposes, the point is that Paul here first commends a woman who is giving significant energy and means to support the church. We should be happy that Phoebe receives so much attention both from Paul and from Christians today, for such attention serves to highlight the value of women in the church, and the beauty of their participation in the servant activities associated with deacons. Whether Phoebe held an official "office" or not, she clearly played a key role in the stability and growth of the early church. Both her role and Paul's public commendation can encourage and instruct the church now.

Next come Priscilla and Aquila, whom we've discussed and whom Paul calls "my co-workers in Christ Jesus" (v 3). Both of them are described this way. The church meets at *their* house (v 5). *They* risked their lives for him, Paul says (v 4). The existence of male leadership in the church obviously neither demands nor allows aloofness or superiority on the part of male leaders or members. We see this clearly when we read these epistles through to the greeting-filled ends, rather than just picking out the hard verses. Paul emerges personally in his greetings, carrying out his leadership with a shepherd's loving care for all his sheep, calling them by name. Just imagine what it meant to each one to have his or her name read aloud and recorded in this way.

Paul mentions the hard work of a number of them: Mary, "who worked very hard for you," (v 6); Tryphena and Tryphosa (perhaps sisters), "those women who work hard in the Lord" (v 12); Persis, Paul's "dear friend … another woman who has worked very hard in the Lord" (v 12). There's a sense of close family in these verses; in fact, Paul sends greetings both to Rufus and to Rufus' mother, who, Paul says, "has been a mother to me, too" (v 13).

These phrases offer glimpses into the energy and community of these first-century Christians scattered throughout an empire where often they were not welcome, but where the gospel was bearing fruit on every side through their lovingly-shared labors. We believers today can identify with them, and learn from them.

We skipped over verse 7:

> *Greet Andronicus and Junia, my fellow Jews who have been in prison with me. They are outstanding among the apostles, and they were in Christ before I was.*

The phrase "outstanding among the apostles" (NIV) has also been taken to mean "well known to the apostles" (ESV). However, both NIV and ESV Study Bibles note that the meaning is not that these two joined the rank of Paul and the twelve originally called out; either they were "highly esteemed" by the apostles, or they were apostles according to the more general meaning of "messengers of the gospel"—like missionaries. They were most likely a married couple who were involved together in spreading the gospel, and who suffered in prison with Paul for doing so.

Carry It Forward

Scripture abounds with challenging glimpses of women playing crucial and active roles side by side with men, in a church where there is God-ordained order, and within that order a shared life and mission. The women are right in the thick of it: praying... prophesying... learning... teaching... working hard in the Lord... partnering with and encouraging leaders... serving as missionaries... providing financial support... opening up their homes... suffering imprisonment... mothering... the list could stretch on. The picture is a vibrant and beautiful one, because it is a picture of the body of Christ. Only with Christ as our head can we men and women made in his image join together to worship and serve our Creator God.

The implications of this picture are as varied as the examples in it. The main implication is a call for women and men to follow the lead of these early saints in loving and giving our lives to the church, until we see Christ face to face. We get to carry it forward. Through the living picture of Christ's body we are called to bear witness together to a world full of people who need to know him. The picture is not perfect yet, as it will be. But it's Christ's picture, his church—and we get to be in it. Through his Spirit we can live out the kind of love that will draw other women and men into the family of God. As we grasp this bigger picture of God's growing family, our chafing at God's order is gradually replaced with a sense of privilege—and joy—at being a part of it. This is beautiful truth: we actually get to live and serve in God's family, forever.

This is where God was heading, in Eden. The end of the story brings healing from the brokenness of sin that long ago invaded God's good creation. The whole Bible tells of God creating a people for himself; this is finally accomplished in a church bought with the blood of Christ—his body, his bride. Our part of the story is one in which the church is growing fast, as people stream to him from all the nations, heading toward that day when he will come again.

The Goodness of God

We've glimpsed the Bible's big story, and the consistent goodness of God toward his female imagebearers from beginning to end. As we live out our present part of the story, however, it can get messy. Believers are not done with sin and suffering until we die and enter God's presence or until Jesus comes again.

Women in particular continue to suffer the effects of the fall that began way back there in Genesis. In the last two contexts we've considered, marriage and the church, we can discern both the greatest signs of hope and the worst brokenness of sin. It's not surprising that the serpent Satan would attack most viciously these two structures through which God shines forth the beauty of Christ and his redeemed people. That's what Satan began to do in Eden—and he lacks the creativity to think up other methods.

All this means that we male and female human beings must trust unswervingly in God's word to light the way to the end. It's been the goal of this book to point to the light of that word—which, in the end, is the light of Christ our Savior. As his followers, we walk in his light, and that light is good. When Christ appears for a second time, to judge all and to dwell with his people, his light will banish all the darkness forever. On the way to that day, let's affirm God's goodness. Let's know God's goodness deeply, and let's show it clearly.

In light of all we've seen in this book, let's draw three conclusions about how we know God's goodness to women right now, as we live out this part of the story and speed toward the day of Christ's coming.

1. God's Goodness Through His Word

This is not too surprising a first point! *God's people taste his goodness as they take in his word.* The Scriptures are God's breathed-out voice to us—what we were created to feed on and share with others. Particularly in regard to gender issues, voices near and far call us to question God's word, to treat it as antiquated, to reshape it according to our experience, or just to disregard it as our final and sufficient guide to faith and practice. The farther we get from God's word, the less we know his goodness to us.

So, how do we stay close to the word, relishing and sharing God's good revelation? We trust that word supremely—not our own wisdom, not words in a book like this one, or a blog, or anywhere else. We pray and study and seek by God's Spirit to submit ourselves to his authoritative word. We read that word, God-breathed book by God-breathed book. We check one part of the Scriptures with another, and another, from beginning to end. As we study, we lean not only on the Spirit who inspired the words, but also on the community of God's people around us. We sit regularly and humbly under the preaching and teaching of the word, and we seek the counsel of pastors and leaders and friends. We're ready to be corrected. We read the writing of wise thinkers past and present, and we submit all words to the bright light of Scripture. We share God's word in every context where God gives us opportunity. It's an ongoing process, carried out by God's people by God's grace.

For churches, the primacy of God's word points to the importance of biblical training for members. The senior pastor under whom I worshiped and learned for the greatest part of my adult years gave his congregation the gift not just of strong preaching, but also of robust training courses in studying and communicating the Scriptures. Developed and taught by church pastors and elders, these courses were open to women and men. They were rigorous and rich, and they helped train up the congregation in studying and sharing God's word—and in following the Savior at its center. They also helped identify both male and female leaders for various areas of the church.

Deep grounding in the word must become the good thing we can't live without. With voices of challenge loud around us, we must be able to articulate clearly and biblically what we believe and why we believe it. The fact that the pastor/elder role is reserved for qualified men obviously doesn't mean women in a congregation should sit back and simply receive truth. It also clearly doesn't mean we should strive bitterly, resenting God-ordained differences. It means that, alongside the men in our churches, we are positioned to grow and minister with joy—just like so many women in the pages of Scripture.

This may mean speaking, praying, and working with pastors and/or elders to help make teaching and training available for women in a congregation.[31] Along with establishing in-church courses, church leaders might

---

31 Carrie Sandom contributed a helpful chapter on the importance of training leaders in the local church in *Word-Filled Women's Ministry: Loving and Serving the Church*, ed. Gloria Furman and Kathleen Nielson (Crossway, 2015), pages 64-86.

encourage women and men to participate in various workshops or courses of biblical study available outside the church or online. Focused church groups might be established; I know of one pastor who, along with a few experienced women in his congregation, personally trained groups of older women in order to help equip them to mentor younger women according to God's word. A prerequisite for the training was that each of these older women would commit to meeting regularly with a younger woman for a time, aiming to nurture her in the faith. That example might involve a bit more structure than some would enjoy—but it is certainly one with wonderful and unusual pastoral care!

Such training bears good fruit in the life of a church, as women pass on to others what they've learned and are learning. It equips women for effective witness inside and outside the church—in all the contexts and callings of their lives. It would be a shame if men in the church were threatened by biblically- and theologically-trained women; one pastor friend recently told me how much he values such women among his congregation, as they help nurture others personally where men sometimes cannot—and they provide some of the most thoughtful sermon feedback and theological discussion. Women can aim to be this kind of rich word-centered help in a church body. How might an individual woman begin to foster this kind of culture, or help it gain momentum? Well, progress might begin through the prayer-infused conversation of a few women and a pastor, or perhaps through a few women who read the Bible one to one with a few others.

How do we know God's goodness to women now? God's goodness overflows to every one of his created beings through his living and active word.

2. God's Goodness in Christ Jesus

We cannot talk about God's goodness through his word apart from his goodness manifested in Christ himself, who shines forth from that word from beginning to end. *Christ's body knows his goodness through shared connection to Christ our head.* If we search the Scriptures without finding Christ, we're in danger of being like those religious leaders of Jesus' day, to whom he said:

> *You study the Scriptures diligently because you think that in them you have eternal life. These are the very Scriptures that testify about me, yet you refuse to come to me to have life. (John 5 v 39-40)*

It's easy to argue over issues and texts without personally confronting the reality of Jesus. As believers we affirm that reality, and yet we too often are not consciously celebrating the presence of our exalted, risen, reigning Lord Jesus. He is at God's right hand right now, in all his glory; he is with us and in us through his powerful Spirit; and he will burst on our vision soon, with all his glory uncovered. Those facts should loom large in our life together. And yet I know I'm capable of arguing about Jesus and forgetting he's right there. I'm capable of asking if God is good while somehow looking right past his goodness that is poured out to us in his Son.

In chapter 8 of this book I told you about a woman who struggled to love Jesus because he was a man. This woman was working wholeheartedly to achieve all sorts of things for women, especially among Christians: opportunities for education and service, equal respect, the ending of all kinds of insensitivity and abuse. These things are valuable—things we should all aim for. Separate from worship of the Lord Jesus, however, these things become causes, or ends in themselves. They become measuring sticks for human interaction, dividing the "enlightened" people from the "unenlightened." They become strivings for the "empowerment of women"—a phrase we so often hear. It is worth asking the question: does that phrase resonate with the Scriptures?

What does resonate with all we've seen in the Scriptures is that women are to be valued as God's image-bearers along with men—and that all believers, filled and empowered with the Spirit of the risen Christ, together serve him until he comes again. God's ordering of male and female in marriage and in the church is meant to bring about unity. Unity through complementarity. Becoming one, ultimately with Christ and in Christ. Being the unified people of God is our eternally good identity, and we're growing into that identity right now, reflecting Jesus more and more.

This unity of male and female with God and with each other was broken back in Eden, with consequences that stretch through the history of civilization and of the church, to this day—including the mistreatment of many women by many men. The world's solution to that evil is to raise up women apart from men—to empower them. This separate empowerment cements and even broadens the divide between men and women that began at the fall. God's solution to that evil is to call both men and women to bow before him. His good plan is that his called-out people be saved by grace, through faith in Christ—and in Christ, then, we are all raised up together: "God raised us up with Christ and seated us with him in the heavenly realms in Christ Jesus" (Ephesians 2 v 6).

Paul speaks these truths to "us": the body of Christ. Yes, we know him as individuals; we women experience his care just as personally as did those women from the Gospels for whom he stopped crowds, whom he touched, and whom he looked in the face and addressed with words that still move us. And, yes, we will aim as women to nurture the growth of women and the growth of the church in its care for women in particular. But we'll be spurred on by a larger motive: the glory of Christ our head, as that glory is reflected in his body, the church—"us." We'll be motivated to pray for and submit to the leadership of the local congregation of which we are a part. We're going to be out for the health and growth of the body of Christ—and the privilege of shining his light together to the world around.

This truth of our identity as Christ's body should lead us to take great care as we plan for "women's ministry"; if we're not careful, it can separate out the women, put their ministry in a silo, and actually diminish their importance by isolating their participation in the body. In some cases, in the name of honoring women, it seems the women are set aside safely in a separate group devoted to "women's activities," partly to bypass the hard work of integrating a congregation of men and women in service to Christ our head. We simply end up with parallel but not truly partnering populations within the church. It's not just women or men who lose; ultimately we end up diminishing the reflection of Christ's glory, if we do not reflect that glory in robust unity. Even while ministering effectively among women, the women within a church body can help foster unity by seeking to participate actively in the life of the church, for example in prayer, various small groups, areas of financial oversight, teaching, music, curriculum and editorial work, hospitality, children's ministry, mercy ministry, and on and on.

How do we know God's goodness to women now? God's goodness overflows to every part of his body through shared connection to Christ our head.

3. God's Goodness on the Line

Christ's image-bearers know God's goodness through humility before God's word. The book of James tells us to "humbly accept the word planted in you, which can save you" (James 1 v 21). A humble acceptance of God's word means a Spirit-empowered receiving of God's word without adding to it or taking away from it—a process we're going to talk about as "staying on the line."

In the Charles Simeon Trust workshops for women that I sometimes help teach, we have one instruction called "Staying on the Line."[32] It's all about staying on the line of Scripture: not leaving out parts we don't like, and not adding parts we think are needed—like the Pharisees in Jesus' time tended to do, with all their extra rules. *Not* staying on the line is nothing new. It's what Eve did in Eden, when she told the serpent that God had said not to eat the fruit of that tree, *nor to touch it*. Eve went above the line; then she let go of the line. She lost the lifeline of God's word.

It is so easy to want to say more or less than God said, particularly about issues relating to women. If a biblical instruction seems too hard for me—for example, Paul's instruction to Timothy that a woman should not teach or exercise authority over a man—I instinctively look for ways to dodge that line. I go below the line if I diminish the import of those words, perhaps explaining them away as culturally bound though they are linked in Scripture with truths from creation. I go above the line if I use those words to forbid all teaching and leadership of women in the church. In the process of searching out the line of Scripture, it helps to remember that we're talking not about a line of judgment but about a lifeline! We're

---

32 www.simeontrust.org

talking about hearing and following the voice of God that graciously reveals to us the path of life opened to us through his Son. And so we can pray with the psalmist, "Lead me in the path of your commandments, for I delight in it" (Psalm 119 v 35, ESV).

Let's consider two examples of teachings within the larger body of Christ, each of which has a positive thrust that seems, however, to go above the line of Scripture. First, some women have been taught that they should never work outside the home. This rule has been applied sometimes to all wives, sometimes just to mothers with children at home. I've heard of its being applied to all women in general—in which case unmarried daughters would remain in their parents' home and help keep it. It seems this teaching developed through inferences drawn from various biblical texts: especially from Genesis 3, where after the fall Eve is told of painful childbearing to come, and Adam of painful work out in the fields. And then of course there's Titus 2, where we saw the emphasis on women being "busy at home."

There is no doubt that women are the ones privileged to bear children, as God chooses to grant them. There is no doubt about Scripture's emphasis on the priority of home and family. There is no doubt that a husband is called to serve and love his wife as her head, and that she is to submit herself to him with respect, helping him in every way possible. There is no doubt that children should honor their parents. As families work out these clear biblical principles under God and in the church community, fellow believers should cry out encouragement—for the infinitely valuable labor of women who work hard caring for home and children... for that of men who work hard to support and lead their families... and for all the women and men who work hard in a combination of venues. I find no clear rule in Scripture that prescribes only stay-at-home work for women or mothers; surely the priority of their families, as God grants them, can be maintained through a variety (and perhaps a changing variety) of work configurations managed by each family. We should be careful not to go above the line of Scripture in these matters.

The second example involves the definition of masculinity and femininity: that is, aiming to state just what is the essence of manhood or womanhood as God intended it. This aim is made challenging by the fact that Scripture never goes so far as to define manhood or womanhood. We have to extrapolate from what Scripture does say, much of what we've looked at together in this book. Personally, I think it is fascinating and often helpful to try to define these things by extrapolating from Scripture— but I would never want to present my definitions, or anybody's, as explicit teachings of Scripture. That would be going above the line.

Simply emphasizing the starting points that Scripture gives (that is, staying on the line) seems like the best option. In relation to women, several starting points appear clear. We discussed one of them in chapter 7 and have referred to it repeatedly: God made women to carry in themselves the potential to conceive and bear children. Whether or not a woman becomes a mother, the biological equipment related to this potential marks her as a woman, in God's plan. All women experience this mark of womanhood, think a great deal about it, feel hope and pain through it, and muse on the mystery of it. In this sense, "childbearing" is one most basic starting point of womanhood, meant to point us to Christ. Humbly receiving this truth about ourselves from Scripture is staying on the line. Teaching anyone that actually bearing children is the ultimate fulfillment of womanhood would be going way over it—and in fact losing it.

What about the starting point of being a "helper" (see chapter 2)? Was this role given to Eve as the first wife, or as the first woman? The Bible doesn't answer clearly. We've seen the New Testament directives to wives—which, interestingly, don't reference the helper role. Submission is related to helping, but it's not exactly the same thing. In light of Scripture's whole trajectory, it makes sense that the helper role is given to Eve as the first woman, representing the women (not just the wives) to follow her. Adam and Eve's human relationship images the Godhead not just through marriage but, as we've seen, through its picture of the unity of God's people serving him together—a picture that culminates in the church. The line stretches throughout Scripture. In that sense Adam and Eve were the first little congregation of a church plant, with Adam leading and Eve coming alongside as a partner in the work.[33] If this is correct, then the "helper" role is indeed a starting point for all women. Again, it's important to say that in regard to living out that helper role, the Bible gives explicit commands only for the contexts of marriage and the church. But that's no limited application, for the church is the context that lasts forever.

One more starting point for womanhood is not a specific directive but rather a cluster of words—words like submission and quietness. These qualities are to characterize all God's people, but we see these words repeatedly associated with women in the New Testament. 1 Timothy especially emphasizes quietness: that verse about not teaching or exercising authority is encased in a call to "quietness

---

33 I first heard this idea from David Helm, Lead Pastor at the Hyde Park congregation of Holy Trinity Church, Chicago, and Chair of The Charles Simeon Trust.

and full submission" (1 Timothy 2 v 11) and a call to "be quiet" (v 12). There's a restraint urged here: a quietness not just of mouth but also of spirit, as women submit to church leadership and ultimately to God. The preceding verses exhort women to modesty in worship, urging a similar sense of restraint:

> *I also want the women to dress modestly, with decency and propriety, adorning themselves, not with elaborate hairstyles or gold or pearls or expensive clothes, but with good deeds, appropriate for women who profess to worship God. (v 9-10)*

Paul urges women toward an outward appearance that is not "loud," but that matches a humble and worshipful inner being.

A line begins to appear. The same cluster of concepts appears in 1 Peter 3, addressing wives but with principles applicable to all women:

> *Your beauty should not come from outward adornment, such as elaborate hairstyles and the wearing of gold jewelry or fine clothes. Rather, it should be that of your inner self, the unfading beauty of a gentle and quiet spirit, which is of great worth in God's sight. (1 Peter 3 v 3-4)*

Both passages climax with a focus on God—worshiping him, living in his sight. This is the point: living in worship of the Lord God. That's the line we want to stay on. Both passages call women not simply to a list of outward rules but to an inward quietness of spirit before God that evidences itself in outward restraint of words, dress, and behavior.

Have you known women who have a quiet spirit? This doesn't mean weak women; it means the strongest ones, who exercise restraint over themselves as by the Spirit they submit themselves to God and to his word. Think of the women in Romans 16. Such a spirit is not what the world today generally celebrates in women. Such a spirit characterizes an effective helper; it strengthens and lifts up those around her. It shines through a glorious array of personalities and gifts. It leads to amazing accomplishments and fulfillment without self-promotion. It shines a unique witness in a world that has thrown off restraints. A quiet spirit is worth our prayerful consideration, as one of the starting points for godly womanhood.

Showing off the Goodness of God

We've summarized the ways in which we know God's goodness to women right now: by his word; in Christ our head; and through humility before God's word as we read and "stay on the line." What remains for us is to live in a way that shows off that goodness. Before a world that often scorns God's revelation, let us not respond by retreating. Let us not teach the Bible's truths with embarrassment. Rather, may we speak and live them humbly and boldly, aiming first and foremost to bear witness to God's goodness to us in Jesus Christ his Son.

The biblical truths about women point us relentlessly to Jesus. They are not truths to be taught as rules, for their own ends. They may well not be the first truths we share with those who don't yet know Christ. They are most beautiful not when they're plucked out of the Bible and turned into a teachable system, but rather when they are encountered as part of the whole revelation of God's word, and lived out among God's people. We can scatter hints of these beautiful truths by the way we live as women and men in unity together under the lordship of Christ.

We must not pretend that we do this, or ever have done this, perfectly. Far from it. It is crucial that we in the church, men and women together, admit openly the ways we have failed to live out God's goodness. We can repent and confess to one another, as fellow sinners cleansed by the blood of Christ and depending on God's grace. We can show each other and the world what forgiveness looks like. We can pray for ourselves and for one another in the various callings and responsibilities God has given us in home and church and society, and we can aim to partner together in the gospel more and more wholeheartedly, so as to spread that gospel to those around us.

The gospel is the good news of a good and glorious God who has redeemed his creation through his Son. May we redeemed women and men live to show off God's goodness, for the glory of Christ, until he comes again.

Acknowledgments

I'm overwhelmingly grateful to the Lord God for a life full of loved ones and friends who have taught me and lived out before me the truths celebrated in this book. My father died before the book was completed, but he prayed for it and cheered for it—just as he did for every single task I have ever tackled. Dad taught the word and ministered to people according to the word, at work and at home and everywhere he found himself, to the end. He had two daughters, one now in heaven along with him, and he encouraged us both to press ahead with joy in service to the Lord Jesus. I praise God for the gift of a father and mother who together passed on spiritual riches in Christ, and who showed my sister and me the importance of passing them on.

I'm grateful for the faithful churches of which I've been a part, where I've witnessed the body of Christ working out many of the issues this book addresses. Pastor Kent Hughes, at College Church in Wheaton, Illinois, was for many years a godly shepherd to our whole growing family; he fostered a church-wide growth in the Scriptures that left its mark on many lives, including mine. As I've worked on this book, I've sat for part of the time under my husband's preaching in Jakarta, Indonesia, and for part of the time under our son's preaching in Roselle, Illinois. God is growing and strengthening his church on all sides of the globe; what an encouragement to see God's hand on his people near and far as I've considered questions so fundamentally important to relationships in the church.

The folks at The Good Book Company have been consistently encouraging and thoughtful in all their help and input—as well as my cohorts at The Gospel Coalition. It's been a joy to work closely with Mary Willson in TGC's women's initiatives during the writing of this book. Mary prayed, listened, advised, and read parts of the manuscript along with Ann Westrate; I'm grateful for their help and encouragement. Gloria Furman read some and prayed a lot. Don Carson took the time amid all his travel and work to read through a draft and offer feedback. I am blessed by such friends.

And I am blessed by the great gift of a loving family. Jon and Jeanne, Dan and Lyndee, and David—thanks for discussing, praying, and always encouraging. First and foremost, and finally, loving thanks to my husband Niel, who read and re-read, who sees clearly and speaks straight, and who always calls me on ahead to discover more.